Beyond the Locked Door

By

Betty Kossick

*For
Wylma Jensen
Joy in Jesus!
Betty Kossick*

1

Library of Congress Cataloging-in-Publication Data

Published by BookSurge Publishing LLC, an Amazon.com Company
Printed in the U.S.A.

Betty Kossick
bkwrites4u@earthlink.net

Beyond the Locked Door
ISBN # 1-4196-5311-3

Reorder at the following addresses:
www.booksurgepublishing.com
www.amazon,com
www.borders.com

•·

In Appreciation
And
Dedication

When this little book started in its infancy formation, the preview readers saw it in stages of development. The process proved rather like the sonogram of a baby's growth in the womb. Each reader's critique, prayers--and encouragement served as my buoys to complete the task. I placed this book on a shelf for a while to be co-author of another book. That time, a combination of hard work as well as repast, aided me as I returned to this book, to see it through to its birth.

There are too many readers to list all your names but you all know how I value each of you. Christians, a Jewess--and those of no religious persuasion did the reading. Some of you wanted me to write a very detailed book, I chose not to do this. As one of the readers, my friend from high school days, Louise Moss, advised me, "A book is only as long as it takes to tell the story." Wise advice. I took it.

To all of you who urged, "Your story must be told," here it is with special thanks to my dear husband Johnny, who faithfully proofed each chapter. God bless him!

This book is dedicated to the Giver of gifts, my Father God, His Son Jesus and the Sweet Holy Spirit

Preface

Many of those born into a personal world of abuse, ignorance and pain grow up to be more dysfunctional and violent than the parents who reared them

Others, including Betty Kossick, are like calla lilies, drawing only good from the swamp about their roots and blooming tall and lovely

Betty is a gentle, greatly-loved lady who appreciates beauty, daintiness and flowers, even flowered wallpaper, which the sight of frightened her for years. The story of her life tells you why

It goes on to tell how a loving heavenly Father healed her longing for a caring father of her own—and lifted her above the morass of the past to dwell in the pure light of love and service to Him. It was Betty who coined the Dayton Christian Scribes motto: "Writing for God's glory."

She has lived it, written it, and spoken it. This book is her testimony.

Lois Pecce
Co-founder (with Betty) of Dayton Christian Scribes
Dayton, Ohio

Table of Contents
for
Beyond the Locked Door

Mommy and me

Though this story begins with this little girl's cheerless memories, read on and you will discover her joyful life as an adult

Chapter I

"A FAMILY LOST"

"... I do remember that I felt very grown up. I could turn a key and open a door!"

For years, I cringed in rooms with flowered wallpaper. Trapped. The snare, a scene I've always wanted to wish away.

A weather-beaten, dilapidated house provided my mother, my father and myself a home, when I was a child of five. Actually our part of the home consisted of only one small room, an upstairs bedroom papered with floral design.

The walls of our room hung empty, which signified our unhappy life. My parents sub-rented this room, in Akron, Ohio, during the mid-1930s from a large, indigent family who occupied the first floor and part of the second. Our room smelled dank–as did the rest of the house. The smell grew worse when I walked into the hallway near the bedrooms of my young friends, dominated by the pungent odor of urine. The best escape from the drabness and the unpleasant smells came with the open screenless window, even ignoring the pesky flies. The late summer breezes brought in the fragrance of ripening grapes from an aging, neglected arbor.

The mister who lived downstairs and my father were drinking buddies. Daddy and his friend never handled their liquor well. One night in that room, with the flowered wallpaper, my father beat my mother almost senseless in a drunken rage. My mother obviously feared such an act, because she said to me, earlier that day, in a note of nervous anticipation, "Betty Ann, you need to learn how to unlock doors."

She taught me how to use a skeleton key to turn the lock. When I did it correctly, she praised, "Good, Snooks. But this will be our secret. Don't tell Daddy that you know how to do this." I don't recall asking one of those "whys" a five-year old might ask about the secretiveness --but *I do remember that I felt very grown up. I could turn a key and open a door!*

Daddy and the mister reeled home drunk that night, while I played downstairs with my friends. Mommy often indulged in the reading of romance magazines. Probably, she was lying on the bed upstairs reading the latest issue of *Modern Romance.* I didn't have many toys but I loved my little yellow rocker. I enjoyed sitting in my very own chair, cradling my cat, Fluffy, and rocking him like a baby. The family allowed me to keep my rocker in their sparsely furnished living room downstairs. My friends and I always tried to ignore our tipsy daddies. Though their raucous behavior gave us children frequent cause to tremble, most of the time we adapted quite well to their obnoxious actions.

That night my Daddy's frightening behavior escalated dangerously. After urinating on our friend's sofa, as though it were a toilet, he turned and in a furious outlash started kicking at my little rocker, yelling and cursing, "I told you to keep your toys put away!" He stomped again and again on my precious rocker until only a heap of yellow wood shards and pieces remained. I sobbed for my smashed rocker, as my little-girl heart broke. Unable to grasp his rage, fear seized me. Yet he clutched more fury to come.

My father stumbled up the stairs with me in tow. Tears streaming, I watched him lock the door of our room. Immediately, a cursing, screaming scenario ensued between my Daddy and my Mommy. His hands started to harm my

Mommy, just like his foot hurt my rocker. The sounds of hard slaps and thuds combined with damning yells, and retorting shrieks permeated the room. *Is my Daddy going to kill my Mommy?* I knew better than to beg, "No, no" or plead in any way. Because of my exposure to hearing curse words every day, the ugliest of words filled my mind, though I didn't know what they meant, I knew they meant something bad—very bad. I applied them to my father—and wanted to yell those words at him. Now, he seamed like a wild beast, not a Daddy. And I knew enough to be mute. Though almost jaded, due to previous family curse-and-scream fights, this time terror gripped me completely. How does one explain the agony, unless ones feels it?

My thin chest tightened from the rapid beating of my heart. Desperate to find help, I edged along the wall to the door, turned the key, the door unlocked! I grasped the cold marble doorknob and I hurried down the creaky, dark, narrow flight of stairs, hollering for the missus to "Get the cops, quick!" Gaunt in appearance with a bulging belly, she wiped her flushed face with the back of her hand, as she put her arm around me, "It's gonna be okay," she sighed. In those days, few people in our neighborhood possessed a telephone, so unless you lived next to a police station, it took time to get law enforcement help.

The missus cautioned me, "Stay downstairs here, youngun' until the officers arrive. I'll get your Momma help." Her scared kids fled the house during the turbulence. So I indulged in my warranted tears all the more, as I took refuge under a table. I felt abandoned. By the time the police arrived, my father's snoring sounded throughout the small house. The missus snorted, "It's something how these drunks can sleep like li'l babies after a binge, even when they act like the Devil hisself." Saying that, she glared with disgust toward the bedroom where her husband also fell into a snoring sleep, never waking during the entire turmoil.

Then, we heard my Mommy pleading from the upstairs communal bathroom, where she'd huddled, "Please, please get me a doctor."

All the ugly bedlam reminded me of previous times when my parents also fought in another house that had a built-in floor-level bookcase with glass doors. At age three or four I used to hide inside that bookcase with my cat, Fluffy, whispering to him, "Fluffy, no one will find us here." I'd squeeze my eyes shut, thinking that made us invisible to anyone. I'd stop my ears with my fingers to shut out the chaos but I still heard the painful words. I remember trembling and wanting a hug instead of the fear.

But now at this house, I found no place to hide except under a small table in the corner of the kitchen A suffocating feeling gripped me. Tears ran down my face and plopped on the linoleum-covered floor, while I scooted as far as possible toward the back of the table against the wall— and I heard a siren.

Two policemen rushed in, and at a hand gesture of the missus, they tromped up the stairs and hauled my father out of bed. He weaved down the stairs mumbling, "Whasamatter? Whachadoin'?" They guided him into the police car. "Off to jail with you, you no good wife-beater," one of the officers snarled, while wielding his nightstick. By this time, I'd scrambled from my hiding place under the table and hid behind the open front door—watching. In a panic, the missus dashed again to beg the use of a telephone at a neighbor's house to call for medical help.

After a while, a heavy-set doctor arrived to treat my Mommy. He gently advised me, "Curly top, you stay downstairs. I'll help your mother." After awhile, he lumbered down the stairs. He spoke hushed words to the missus. Then, he came over to me and squatted his large frame down to my level, where I'd returned to hiding, scrunched under the table whimpering. He wooed me out and patted me on the head before he left. As he unwrapped a stick of Juicy Fruit gum, he said, "Chew this. It will stop your tears." Amazingly it did.

I don't know how my bruised and swollen-faced mother did it physically but the next day she and I walked away from the flowered-wallpaper room. She carried two shopping bags of our belongings, and I held tightly to my squirming cat. We walked several blocks to the duplex home of a friend, another woman who reared four sons alone. She took us in like dropped off, unwanted pups; refugees of domestic violence.

Mommy and our friend talked until late at night. I felt strange in this new place, begging to stay up and afraid to go to bed until my mother did. I listened as Mommy told her friend how my Daddy's previous drunken behavior always found her forgiving him again and again because he urged, "I'm sorry. I promise I'll never do it again." I'd heard it all before. I wanted to stop up my ears. He always insisted that he loved her, pleading, "You're the love of my life." Previously, she'd even forgiven him when the police brought me home in the middle of the night, after they took him to jail. They found him holding my four year-old hand while I precariously balanced on the railing of Akron's High Level Bridge. His distorted, drunken stupor nearly cost me my life.

One of the policemen told my mother, "Your old man was staggering drunk." He'd taken me on a drinking spree with him. The other policemen stressed, "Lady, get rid of that guy!" (I heard her repeat that story many times over the years.)

As her friend and I listened, Mommy sputtered angrily, "This time I've made up my mind, no more of his kind of love, no more of him."

I suppose for my Daddy, spending the few dollars he earned for liquor allowed him to forget the poverty of life. A window washer, he worked on highrise buildings. Fearful, he liquored up to get the courage to climb on a scaffold. Yet his escape made us all paupers emotionally and physically.

After a few weeks of living with our friend and her sons, Mommy realized that we couldn't stay any longer. Untrained to do any kind of professional employment, menial jobs were all that she could muster. Actually, to obtain any kind of work during the Great American Depression proved fortunate. Even without a drunk for a husband and father, we were among many money-hurting, often cupboard-bare people. My mother also made another decision: to place me in a children's-care home. "Just for a little while," she promised.

Again we walked together, carrying only a partially-filled shopping bag for me, to a house with a big front porch on May Street. Mommy's friend offered to keep my cat, promising to take good care of him. Regardless, I sobbed. I feared that our friend's big black dog, Thor, might eat Fluffy.

Finally, my parents legally separated. Due to lack of finances, five years transpired before my mother received a divorce from my father. As a result, there were no endearing memories of sitting on a daddy's lap or of him reading bedtime stories to me.

The promise of "just a little while" at the children's care home turned in to five years. At age 10, I went to live with my Mommy again--but never again with my Daddy.

A Family Lost
(poem)

I remember the bookcase
built into the rental-house wall,
with deep shelves and glass doors;
the secret hiding place for my cat and me:
it's where I retreated to escape
to stop my ears and close my eyes.
My age? I guess--about four years old,
I had to be – for it was before the split.

Daddy staggered in, too often liquored;
he cursed,
Mommy, hurt and angered, bickered,
she yelled.

A "soap opera" in living color –
even as a child I knew the ending script.
Payday meant booze money not groceries.
Then, another house with a darker scene.
Finally two thin figures walked away;
I carried my cat,
Mommy carried two shopping bags
and we started over.

by
betty kossick

My early days with Aunt Golda and my "new sisters and brothers." I am the kid in the front row with the curls and the kitten.

Chapter II

"PASSPORT TO HEAVEN"

"Aunt Golda gave me a gift of industry that I applied to many aspects of my life"

The first day I met the new mother figure in my life, apprehension absorbed me. In past weeks everything happened too fast and my young mind whirled. After Mommy left me at the children's care home that day, Aunt Golda, as I was told to call her, asked sternly, "Do you know how to iron your clothes?"

Faking bravado, I looked up at her tall aproned-form, shook my curly-locks head side to side and answered with staunch assertiveness, "I can unlock doors."

She grinned, urging, "That's good. If you can do that, you can iron."

Even though, I was tall for a five-year old, she set up a box for me to stand on at an ironing board--and I started learning from an exacting taskmaster.

"The reason we iron clothes is to get rid of all the wrinkles, so you might as well learn it right," she insisted.

Standing tall and stiff, I obeyed but I thought, *She's an old witch!*

That first night, full of miserable imaginings, I cried and cried until I fell asleep, wondering, *Will I ever see my Mommy again?* I felt like the storybook Gretel. My immature child-like thoughts played havoc, *Will the witch stuff me in an oven?*

As that little insecure child, I didn't realize what a favor my bedraggled mother did for me. Soon I settled in to the home routine; ironing my clothes, and learning other tasks such as washing and drying dishes, broom-sweeping floors, sorting laundry into piles, picking gooseberries—and carefully washing them. I actually enjoyed learning all the homemaking tasks. My night sobs and nightmares ceased.

Though I didn't know it then, the work ethic I acquired benefited me. *Aunt Golda gave me a gift of industry that I applied in all aspects of my life.* The skills also taught me to earn money as a teenager, and later as a young wife and mother to augment family income.

One thing I never got used to—the group Saturday night bath ritual, our only bath of the week. Three or four of us shared the same bath water together, then another group used the water. I vocalized many times, "I want my own bathtub and my own water!"

I also rebelled about going without shoes in the summer time. A squeamish kid, bare feet and I didn't get along. My pleas to wear my shoes went ignored until one day I stepped on a board with a rusty nail. A hospital trip resulted in me obtaining the right to wear shoes in the summer. Also, playing in the mud and mud pie-making turned me off. My friends teased me and called me names like "Miss Prissy" or "Fraidy-cat," but I hated the squishy stuff.

As time passed, Aunt Golda exposed me to an important aspect of my walk through life, one that allowed me to learn to unlock another door--a portal to my spiritual life.

On Sunday mornings Aunt Golda, whom I quickly learned wasn't a witch after all, took us little charges of near-orphans off to the nearby Main Street Methodist Church. In that brick haven, I discovered about the Son of God, named Jesus. I'd learn to be forever grateful to the Methodists for teaching and assuring me that Jesus loves me.

About two years later the Methodists provided me with a passport to heaven. My document: an 8 by 11 inch sheet of paper. The passport held my own picture in one top corner and a picture of Jesus in the opposite corner. For years, I assumed that I must present that passport to enter the heavenly gates. I unfolded and refolded that document often and wondered, *What is heaven really like? What is Jesus really like?* I treasured my passport and kept it in a colorful *White Owl* cigar box someone gave me.

Though still a youngster, I felt more grown up living with Aunt Golda. Often she'd commend, "You're a quick learner." When I saw my parents, I started calling my mother Mom instead of Mommy and my father Dad instead of Daddy.

While living with Aunt Golda, I also wrote my first poem, as a second-grader at Allen School. An unusual Monday morning in April provided the fodder for the poem because heavy snowfall the previous day hardly seemed spring-like. Our teacher asked us to write what we thought of the odd April weather. I wrote a poem, I titled "Make Believe Spring" in large printed letters in my Big Chief writing tablet. My teacher didn't change a word-- and to this day I can recite it. Yet I'd be 40-years old before I realized that a writer resided inside of me—waiting for my time.

I found that teachers, in whatever capacity, played pivotal roles in my life. In elementary school they often looked out for my emotional needs. Such as the times my Mom couldn't come to school programs in which I performed major or minor parts. The teachers saw me crane my neck, hoping for a parent-filled chair in the auditorium. I usually pre-empted my parental void by announcing beforehand, "My mother can't get off work." But I still hoped and searched. I remember the tender hugs my teachers gave me after a recitation or a play.

Five years with Aunt Golda passed rather swiftly but during this time, I acquired lots of foster brothers and sisters. Mary already lived with Aunt Golda when I arrived. Tillie arrived shortly after. The three of us were about the same age. Childless, Aunt Golda, who bore no children from her short-lived marriage, eventually adopted Mary, whose own mother died. That's when Mary's surname changed from Zattas to Best, which seemed like such a big thing to me. *How would she ever get used to that?* I thought. Bernadette, a sweet child with a demure smile, died due to a defective heart. Her death saddened us all. Other children, both boys and girls, came and went.

Mom visited frequently, mostly alone but sometimes she brought a new man friend along. I remember the dress she wore when she dressed up to "go out." The lavender, violet and purple crepe fabric enhanced her deep-set blue eyes and dark blonde hair. She looked rich and pretty and seemingly glowed when she wore that dress. When she came alone, her visits usually found me sitting next to her on a sofa, while she told her latest problems to Aunt Golda. However, she'd joke about her hardships, as though laughing at them might make them disappear. The best visits were when she'd take me to see Shirley Temple movies such as *Little Miss Marker*.

My Dad occasionally came to see me too. Sometimes he also brought a new woman friend along. In a sober state, my Dad seemed pleasant and always requested, as he bent over, "Give your Daddy a kiss." Little did he realize that I yearned for him to sweep me up in his arms and give me the kiss—but he never did. With dark, European coloring and a tall, slender build, I thought, *My Dad is good looking.* I really wanted him to be like a knight in shining armor. But I never saw his armor or a white horse.

One summer, after I turned nine years old, Aunt Golda told me that a family wanted me to visit them. "You'll be going on a short vacation," she told me. I'd never been on a vacation, so the idea sounded good to me. I'd heard that vacations were fun times. The family lived in the countryside near a large lake. Canoes, rowboats and motorboats glided on the waterways, while people ate at picnic tables along the shore. When I saw this lovely environment, it all seemed like a fairyland to me.

The man and woman were the parents of one child; a teenage daughter named Dorothy, who enjoyed some local fame as an award-winning swimmer. Dorothy spoiled me. She allowed me to play with her precious outgrown toys: little china dishes, a beautiful child-size cupboard, and a baby doll in a cradle and carriage. Her feminine bedroom, with a dressing table, skirted with pink gossamer ruffles, enthralled me. On top of it sat a row of nail polish bottles.

These bottles of various colors fascinated me, including one of black nail polish. I giggled as she polished my fingernails--and my toenails. *She's treating me like a kid sister,* I thought. I didn't know it until later but that's exactly why I was there. The family hoped to adopt me. They indeed wanted me to be Dorothy's sister. But my mother determined that she and I would eventually get a place of our own and live together again. Her answer was, "No." Regardless, I hold good memories of my "vacation."

Shortly after this experience, Mother moved into Aunt Golda's large home, renting a room. However, I continued staying in one of the bedrooms with the other children. A recent addition to Aunt Golda's home also made it possible for her to harbor yet more children. That new larger room outfitted with bunk beds, caused most of the kids to vie for one of those, they especially wanted the top bunk, but I didn't hanker for one of those at all; I was afraid that I'd fall out.

A year later Mother told me, "Your Dad and I are legally divorced now. We'll make it on our own. I've found an apartment for us to move into." Since I was officially a ward of the Children's Services, she had to get that approval as well, and she did.

However, our new home turned out to be another one-room abode. My Dad visited sometimes but when he did he always smelled of liquor--and sometimes so tipsy that he only muttered. A few months later we heard that he and another drinking chum were jailed for stealing a cigarette machine during a drunken spree. Though my respect for him waned more and more, I still hoped that he'd be a real Dad to me. Yet during the six months of his confinement in the county jail, I walked about four miles, round trip, every Saturday to visit him. Mom carried on every Saturday, "You have no business going there!" but when she went off to work, I went anyway. I reasoned in my mind, *Dad must feel lonely in jail.* I felt sorry for him.

The first time I visited the jailhouse my heart pounded with fright. Subsequent visits didn't lessen the trepidation much because all inmate's visitors were carefully scrutinized. When the heavy iron door clanged shut behind me I really wondered each time if I'd get back out. I've never considered myself a risk-taker but I guess I possessed a certain amount of pluck in my new role as a latch-key kid.

My Dad always looked embarrassed when I came to the jail to see him. Thinking back, I'm sure that he probably wished that I'd stayed home but I hoped to help him somehow. I always showed a helper's spirit as a child. Was this a part of it? I guess. He never said much, just a few awkward words like, "How are you doing kid?"

or "Does your mother know you're here?" "Or did you walk all the way here?" I felt self-conscious, too, and I'll admit that relief flooded me when visitation time ended. Why did I keep going back to suffer through the old proverbial "glutton of punishment" scene? Why did a 10–year old make such a choice week after week? All I can answer in retrospect is that my innate want of a whole family connection drove me. I still wanted a real Dad.

In the meantime Mom and I started a succession of frequent address moves. Our third apartment was the other side of a revamped poultry store. Just a few nights after we moved there, on December 7, 1941, newspaper hawkers called out, "America at War" and "Japs Attack Pearl Harbor." Because not every family owned a radio, clusters of folks tuned in and listened communally to hear President Franklin Roosevelt speak of that terror, the day he dubbed "the day of infamy" when World War II began. Neighbors flocked together in the streets, and on front porches, shocked at the news. A teenage neighbor fellow, probably about 18, yelled, "I'm going to war. Who wants to come with me? We'll get 'em."

Before the war news broadcast that evening, I'd been working diligently on an art project for school, using a cigar box, large buttons, pipe cleaners, cotton, bits of fabric, paint and glue. I worked hard to make all that stuff look like a farm wagon, filled with cotton pickers, depicting the Old South. I started questioning my mother, "Will bombs start falling on us too? Will we die" And other thoughts went through my mind, *What if I can't take my project to school?! My teacher will be disappointed. I won't get a good grade.*

Mom didn't answer me. Tears streaked her lean face, the first I'd seen her cry since that awful night in the room with the flowered-wallpaper. Her kid brother, Leon, whom she'd never seen since a lonely night when she left Pennsylvania with her own baby, was now a serviceman stationed in Pearl Harbor. "Is he alive or dead?" she questioned aloud.

Yet, for us, the awful war proved to be a blessing because Mom obtained dependable factory work at the Firestone Tire and Rubber Company. I can only imagine what the thought of a regular paycheck meant to her. We'd now exist without being on the dole, for we'd often depended upon the assistance of community help agencies.

Mother never talked to me about any of our problems. She didn't want to explain anything to me. But in my own mind I hoped for no more standing in line for clothing, and other necessities. Something we did frequently, even when I lived with Aunt Golda. I still recall the first time I stood in such a line. Aunt Golda led me to a desk where she released my hand from hers and a smiling lady handed me a navy blue jumper, a white blouse and a flowered nightgown. The same clothing package that every other little girl waiting in that line got. I didn't know the word clone then but it certainly fit the scenario: clothes cloned. I didn't really mind getting the same clothes but I knew that we stood in the "poor" line. I didn't like that.

Yet at Christmastime, a fun line filled up when lots of regular families stood in line for the Firestone Tire and Rubber Company Employee's Christmas party. Oh! such delight! We went to a large auditorium where entertainers put on a stage show and clowns did all kinds of clever, funny acts. Santa gave us all gifts. We heartily sang the songs of the season. Everyone looked and acted happy. The festive, cheerful atmosphere provided reprieve and, I didn't feel irregular; I thought, *I'm like everybody else.*

After my Dad's release from jail, just before

Christmas, he came to see us and asked Mom to remarry him. She refused, telling him that she wanted no part of a jailbird. Disappointment filled me because I'd hoped for us to be a real family again. Many years later I discovered that my Dad also served time in a boy's reformatory school in his teen years. I also found out that his behavior probably resulted from negligence and the worst of role-modeling. His father married several times or lived with women without marrying them, after my Dad's mother died at a young age.

Soon, I'd be grateful that Mom decided not to reconcile with my Dad because he showed up drunk too many times. It seemed that he couldn't encounter us without gathering false courage from liquor. I flinched when he staggered in, talking like a braggart. His whole behavior discomforted me. I got to the point that I wanted to disappear when he came but I mistrusted leaving Mom alone with him. Sometimes I thought, *My Dad is just plain crazy.* Actually, pitiful is a more apt word to describe him because I believe that he really did want to be with us. But the liquor bottle always proved more enticing.

Despite the foul smell that emitted from the other side of our apartment through the poultry store, it meant chicken dinner every Sunday at no cost for Mom and me. Ironically, my Dad never showed up on Sunday. I looked forward to Sundays.

The childless landlord and his wife were good-natured, high spirited-Italians. The wife cooked delicious spaghetti and meatballs and she baked fragrant Italian bread. She taught me how to roll spaghetti with a fork and spoon, to make it easier to eat. Her kitchen provided a happy haven, as she smiled and sang Italian songs, while she cooked.

In recall, I still imagine the delicious smells! My

Mom fried a chicken or roasted a hen and the four of us dined together. The couple seemed like grandparents to me. I savored the kindness of these dear people even more than the food.

The landlady sprayed her apartment with *Evening in Paris* cologne, the sweet fragrance hung heavy. But the scent evoked a good feeling—a safe, taken-care-of feeling, leaving a good memory.

She'd always asked me, "You want some 'Paris' behind your ears?"

I always happily replied, "Yes, please"

The combination of odors in their apartment on Sundays blended to make me consider, *this must be what it's like to be rich*. Full bellies and good fragrance. The laughter and the coziness we shared comforted me.

We enjoyed those Sunday dinners for several months, until the landlord died suddenly. His wife became morose, crying constantly, evading visits. She stopped smiling and quit singing. She cancelled our meal times, feigning illness. I missed our Sundays together. Shortly, the store/apartments were sold--and mother and I packed and moved again.

Chapter III

"STARTING OVER, ONCE AGAIN"

"And there it was! Romans 8:28, it read exactly as the pencil was imprinted."

Living again with mother didn't really solve my kid problems. The sense of difference loomed strong, like the proverbial fifth wheel. My friends with intact families mismatched my life. That is, until in the sixth grade at Lincoln School when I acquired a new friend, Nancy Anderson. Her mother also divorced a drinker. Anna's lot proved challenging too, as she reared three girls.

However; relatives of Nancy's lived in town, people who provided buffers for Anna and her girls: a family connection and emotional support. For Mom and me it seemed mostly--we two--against the world, no grandparents, no aunts, uncles or cousins. For us, no one lived down the street or across town to talk to or run to for hugs. At least at Aunt Golda's we enjoyed gatherings for holidays and other occasions. For Mom and me holidays usually meant walking to or riding a bus downtown to see the latest film at one of Akron's many movie theatres. No family gatherings. An unspoken loneliness prevailed—and a state of depression enveloped Mom when holidays came around, especially at Christmas time. To avoid her gloominess, I'd delve into a book to escape and wish for better.

Throughout these years, I yearned for affection. Mom did too but she pretended not. A sociable person, my mother tended to be a jokester most of the time. But she seldom showed any outward affection for me, certainly not with hugs and kisses. I suppose more than anything the tiredness and the frustration that she faced daily masked her tender feelings and set up an emotional barrier. Quite feisty by nature, I'm sure her scrappy ways added fuel to those bad days in her marriage to my father. I remember well, her fishwife yelling. On the other hand, I'm sure that it was her stiff-upper-lip nature that enabled her to survive those--and continuing difficult times. She'd declare often, " I don't take guff from any one. And don't you let anyone push you around either."

Later I discovered that Mom largely lived a life of pretense, most likely to serve as a shield for her emotions. Before she married my father she'd gone through a previous heart-breaking episode. Three years before my birth, she'd been harshly turned out of her family home with her newborn baby daughter, Ruth. With her own mother's sudden death a few months before and her father's status as a leading small-town businessman, the family chose not to handle the shame that the 1920s society associated with out-of-wedlock babies. Taking pity on his kid sister, an older brother, Don, figured she needed to start over in another place. He drove her from that Pennsylvania hamlet and dropped her off in the middle of the night at a Salvation Army haven in Akron, Ohio. When she walked into the Salvation Army building, just a girl of 16, she carried two bundles: a bag of her belongings and her baby. Her brother wished her, "Good luck." She never saw him again; he died young from alcoholism.

Soon the dreams of rearing the baby she called, "my little bundle of sunshine" fell apart. An older, loving couple took her child to care for--and my mother set out to find work. Her plan: to earn enough money to retrieve her baby. Yet she barely earned enough for her own room and board. Still a teenager, she felt like Cinderella. She tired of always laboring at hardscrabble jobs. So when some new young friends asked her to go along with them to a dance hall at East Market Gardens, she readily joined them for a night of fun.

Early in the evening, a young man spied the pretty blonde and asked her to dance. Mother swooned into his arms, as the tall fellow with brown eyes and curly brown hair held her waist and twirled her around the dance floor. She thought she'd found her Prince Charming A few months later, the two in-love, 19–year olds married at the Summit County Court House. Though pregnant with me, the naïve bride expected a happy-ever-after marriage. Her sweetheart's promises to adopt her "little bundle of sunshine," toddler Ruth, were probably well intentioned for us all to be a family. But the temptress named Liquor intruded too often and with a vengeance ripped such plans to shreds.

Unfortunately, Mother pretended to her sisters, with whom she occasionally exchanged letters, that the three of us, she, Ruth and I lived together as a family. Though they knew about my parents divorce, they didn't know until after Ruth's marriage that another couple adopted her. Nor did they know that I'd lived in a children's care home for five years. They always thought my mother reared her "little bundle of sunshine" and me, "Snooks," together. They were unaware of the extremely tough times we endured.

Mom and I frequently visited a large comfortable house with a swing on the front porch on tree-lined Paris Avenue. Judy, an old, fat and friendly dog always greeted us at the door. Ruth lived there with two kindly, grandparent-age people she called Mom and Dad. Our visits obviously created an uneasy scenario for Ruth, as she'd politely call out a "Hello," then rush off to do something "very important." She retreated to either her lovely bedroom at the upstairs front of the house or the backyard that looked like a park to me. An arbor with climbing roses always caught my attention. Beyond the arbor grew a profuse abundance of vegetables, in a well-tended garden. Ruth's pleasant home atmosphere seemed idyllic to me. I always wanted to run after Ruth but Mom always pulled me back if I tried. "Don't go if she doesn't ask you," she cautioned me.

Almost a carbon copy of my mother in appearance, Ruth possessed the same blue eyes and blonde hair. In addition, her smile added beauty because of her prominent dimples. When I was 10, my height matched hers at age 13 and I grew to be much taller than she. Even as a child, it didn't surprise me that my mother often referred to Ruth as "my pretty grown-up daughter" now instead of referring to her as "my little bundle of sunshine." My ganglyness contrasted with her prettiness and I thought of Ruth as beautiful. Yet I continued to think, *If Nancy's sisters live with her why doesn't Ruth live with us--if she's really my sister?*

Mom never explained. Anytime I inquired, she rebuffed me harshly. My questions were always answered with, "You wouldn't understand" or "You'll understand when you're grown." After awhile, I realized that my Dad wasn't Ruth's Dad. Or even that that nice old man whom she called Dad wasn't her real father either.

My thirteenth spring, the mailman brought me a package with my Dad's name as the sender. As I opened the package, I found a photograph of an adorable baby girl. A note from him informed me that the baby's name was Joanne. He also enclosed a telephone number, requesting that I call him. In the letter he wrote, " I want you to meet your baby sister and your new mother." This incident threw my mother into fitful hysterics, "Who does he think he is with a new wife and baby and he doesn't even pay support for you?" she hissed. She forbade me to go see him and she ordered me to call him and tell him so. A tough call for a kid to make; I trembled as I dialed the telephone, and I can almost still feel the tightness in my throat as I spoke with a restricted voice. I cried after I hung up. I really did want to see this little sister but I didn't say so to Mom.

Again, I saw my mother crying. My mind flashed back to that room with the flowered wallpaper. No doubt, her tears were for our lost family. Or perhaps they were tears of anger, most probably both. *But how strange*, I mused, for even at age 13, I pondered, *I have two sisters and they aren't sisters to each other. It's weird.* I ran to my bedroom to be alone. I remember reading *Aida,* the opera, as a homework assignment. I needed to get my mind off my crazy life.

A few months later, mother's hopes for Ruth coming to live with us were shattered forever. Ruth told Mom, "I'll never call you my Mother. I want Mom and Dad to adopt me." That night I kept waking up to hear Mom sobbing.

After this, little by little, I sought to learn bits and pieces about my mother's fragmented life but most always what I learned came from someone else, not Mom. She didn't want to confide in me; she continued to rebuff my questions. Ruth's adoptive Mom confided in me as I grew older, helping to fill in the puzzle pieces of our scrap-life.

During the adoption process, Ruth, who chose to spell her name with an "e" (as in Ruthe) asked for her given name to be legally changed to that spelling. Her adoptive parents also enrolled her in a girl's finishing school in Kentucky. I've always suspected they made this choice because Mom and I moved two blocks away from their home shortly before the adoption. In fact, the move probably triggered the adoption. Most likely, for Ruthe, our presence provided an uncomfortable proximity.

Life always seemed to be in a disconnected limbo for Mom and me—but a simple gift of a pencil a few months later provided a wonderful hope for my future.

Miss Josephine Aslan, passed out pencils to all her seventh-grade students. They were not the plain green lead pencils usually distributed by the Akron Public Schools. These were attractive pencils with Bible verses imprinted on them. I remember rolling my pencil back to the verse, reading it, rolling it round again and again, and reading it each time. It read, "And we know that all things work together for good to them who love God," Romans 8:28. My 13 year-old mind determined, *I don't believe this is even in the Bible. It's just a bunch of words, God wouldn't say that. All things? My life work for the good? Forget it.*

Regardless, that day after I got home from school I carefully counted the money I'd saved from my baby-sitting jobs: four dollars. I stuffed the bills in my jacket pocket, and hurriedly walked a couple of miles to the variety store on South Main Street. I found and bought my first Bible; a King James Version. I'd never read a Bible before and my curiosity engaged me in reading it on my way back home. A similar habit of mine, when getting a book from the library—I'd start reading it while walking home. *And there it was! Romans 8:28, it read exactly as the pencil was imprinted*: "And we know that all things work together for good to them that love God." *It really is in the Bible. It has to be true. God wouldn't lie. But I don't know God. What's He like? And that place called heaven I have a passport to, what's it like?*

Thrilled with this discovery. I thought and thought on that verse for a long time. And though those words were only part of the verse in Romans 8:28, I realized some years later the profoundness of that verse in its entirety. The full verse served as a personal prophecy for me. Yet it only took a part of the verse to direct me through another door, as I started my quest for God.

Direction

The Word
Teaches, guides,
Finds the heart,
Then—
Tenderly, surely,
Gives new paths.

by
betty kossick

Teenager Betty,
"all grown up"— and discovering
God and life.

Chapter IV

"DISCOVERIES"

"I'd earned my sheepskin and I also embraced a couple of special loves in my life."

When I started high school, I carried dreams in my heart about going to college. I expressed my desire often. I excelled in art and won many contests. Election to school offices gave me personal confidence. Teachers pointed out promise in me--but when I'd come home and tell my mother about these voices of encouragement, she called it all nonsense, "Betty Ann, you have champagne taste with beer money." She'd frown and wave me away.

Though underage, I got a job hand-painting ceramics for Woolworth's. Mom knew the store manager and he arranged for me to work alone in a basement cubicle, away from the customers who might report me, but I often encountered scampering rats. My dimly-lit corner of the store's basement held a ceiling light bulb with a long heavy string to pull for on and off. Ugh! When I completed painting numberless boxes of white ceramics the manager told me, "I'd like you to learn to decorate candy Easter eggs." However, it still required me to work in the basement. I enjoyed that task but I still deplored the rats. I also found out that rats really love candy. When I turned 16, the manager assigned me new tasks where I applied my artistic skills in greater measure as window decorator and sign painter. I really enjoyed this work and I never spied any more rats once I left the basement—but I knew they were still there.

Being best friends with Nancy, during those adolescent and teenage years, gave us both a cheer that we needed. We weren't inclined to sit and wallow about the unhappiness of our younger years. In fact, I can't recall us ever talking about the ugly times. Often our school chums called us *The Sunshine Twins* because we were always in good humor and just about inseparable. As I look back, our closeness seems ironic because as an athletic girl Nancy enjoyed swimming--and she skated on ice with grace. Not me, I feared to put my head under water and just forget about me gaining any balance on ice skates. In addition, I hated winter weather. I thought surely I'd freeze to death, so ice ponds, sledding and other winter sports revealed my wimpy side all the more. The original dud fit me for games and sports because my coordination measured zero. Of all games, volleyball, tennis, badminton and ping-pong showed my lack of coordination the most. I never got any better. Once when I joined a volleyball game as an adult, the other players kindly requested that I bow out of the game.

Even in elementary school I recall my schoolmates shunning me at game time because I couldn't play Red Rover well. The kids on the opposing side knew the break through always came at Betty Ann's site in the line. I'll admit feeling very incapable at game time. No one ever wanted me on their team, so I dreaded "choosing time" during recess or gym classes. I knew that I'd always be the last one chosen. The worst part, for me, is that I never learned to swim either, even though I attended a school with a swimming pool and an instructor, who taught swimming as a part of the physical education curriculum. Three years of lessons resulted in nothing for me! Later as an adult I took a Red Cross beginners swimming class. Still, I never learned. But these days I do aqua-exercise well in pools.

Regardless of athletic incapability, I excelled in the

arts and most academic subjects. My cranium worked much better than my body. And life slowly improved. Though, always, I yearned for the smell of Old Spice, my Daddy's smell. It's hard to explain but I did. Even though Nancy and I shared similar situations without fathers at home, I still felt irregular because of it. Without any doubt, I'm sure that lack of a man at home led me to the next brief step in my life.

By age 16, encouraged by my mother, I accepted a diamond engagement ring from a young man, whom I'd dated for a short time. We planned to marry after my high school graduation. I'd bought into Mom's philosophy of "champagne taste with beer money." I'd forgo college. However, we broke off our engagement much to Mom's dismay and I concentrated on my eventual graduation.

During this same time I also met my little half-sister, Joanne. My mother and I, and my Dad, his wife Sallie, and Joanne all were uncomfortably brought together at a funeral of an uncle whom I never knew existed. I was fascinated about this deceased uncle (my father's uncle at that), who lay in a coffin with a magnificent red, handlebar mustache. His wife threw herself across the casket, petting his mustache and bemoaning that she'd never see him again! She wailed and wailed!

The last time I'd seen my Dad I was 12 years old—except for a brief few minutes once at age 14, when I encountered him at a bus stop in downtown Akron. I wasn't even sure if it was him. I sided up to him and asked, "Are you my Dad?" He looked at me rather astonished and said, "Well, well, Betty Ann, you've grown up kid. Nice to see you, here's a buck." He pushed a dollar bill into my hand and got on his bus. But at the funeral we all acted quiet cordial as if we all were one family. However, I squirmed inside because I knew we weren't and it bothered me. We all play-acted our roles, be nice, just to be nice.

However at 17, I felt smitten with little Joanne--and she obviously adored me from the start. The funeral home encounter started a friendship with Joanne that continued as she grew up. My Mom liked Joanne too, and didn't seem to mind our ensuing relationship. But often I'd still think, *how strange I have two sisters and they aren't sisters to each other.*

June 1949 arrived and I joined the ranks of South High School's alumni. *I earned my sheepskin and I also embraced a couple of special loves in my life*: my on-going search for God and Johnny, a Seventh-day Adventist.

I'd met Johnny on a rain-touched night in April a few weeks before my graduation. My recent confirmation in a Lutheran fellowship provided me the incentive to talk about my newfound beliefs. Since my Methodist church-going days, I'd attended various other churches with friends. However, I always held a curiosity, *why so many different denominations?* My mother wasn't enthusiastic about this search of mine. She reminded me, "Once a Catholic, always a Catholic." I'd been baptized Elizabeth Anna at St. Ignatius church in Cleveland, Ohio, named after my deceased paternal grandmother Elizabeth and her sister, my great-Aunt Anna, who was mid-wife at my birth. Yet they always called me Betty Ann. My parents never addressed me as Elizabeth.

Along the way, I'd developed a great admiration for Martin Luther by reading about the religious upheaval of the Reformation. I thought of the Reformers as courageous men and women. My best friend Nancy was a Lutheran with Swedish ties. During our early high school years I'd attended church with her and joined a Sunday School confirmation class, finishing my preparation before the other classmates. I requested confirmation. Mom adamantly refused to allow me to join with the Lutherans. Again, she reminded me that I'd forever be a Catholic. The strange part is that she didn't attend church and seemed to disdain Catholicism. In fact, she obviously feared it—at least she spoke harshly about the priests, the sisters and the nuns. Often she lamented that her Catholic school-day memories were miserable ones. But she admired the faithfulness of her mother, a devout Catholic, and a mother of eight children, known for her good works in the community. On the other hand, she thought her father to be a smart fellow to hold out as a Protestant and not join her mother's church. "He would have been a miserable Catholic," she harped.

As a threat to my interest in Protestantism, Mom used a weighty intimidation repeatedly, " If you aren't good, I'll send you to live with your Aunt Lorraine and she'll make you be a Catholic." The warning sounded menacing so, of course, her shake down attempts made me think Catholics must be holy terrors. For the most part I proved to be obedient—but I continued to attend other churches--and I never got sent to Aunt Lorraine's.

My sister Ruthe, reared by Christian Science teachings chose the Lutheran faith in her teens, though she attended a different synod than Nancy belonged to. Interestingly, Ruthe and I bonded as friends and sisters, after she went off to the girl's school in Kentucky. She often wrote me letters and sent me little gift packages. Her attentions pleased me. She never told me why she decided to connect with me and accept me as her half-sister but I suppose she wanted to "belong to blood." I surmised that if I joined her church that we'd be real family, so I decided to do that. Mom didn't like the idea but she didn't protest dogmatically about my decision as she had earlier. I'm sure she tempered her feelings by this time because she felt I'd be more connected with Ruthe—and perhaps connecting her to Ruthe better. Again, I took confirmation classes, but I told the Lutheran church pastor, "I'm joining but I'm still searching for God. I still have a lot of unanswered questions. I don't feel spiritually fulfilled yet." A kindly man, he didn't chastise. He seemed to understand my yearning.

Johnny and I got into religion talks soon into our courtship--but I thought he held some strange beliefs. For one, he attended church on Saturday. Second he spoke about a prophet--a woman prophet named Ellen White. Since I was 12-years old I'd been going to all kinds of churches in my God-search but I'd never heard of Seventh-day Adventists before. Johnny, himself, regardless of being a church member, wasn't faithfully following its beliefs. He'd recently been mustered out of the army and during his time in military service he'd picked up unsavory habits, while neglecting his spiritual life in general.

After observing my interest in spiritual things, he admitted that he needed to mend his own spiritual life. He invited me to attend the Adventist Church. Thus, I'd take a bus across town and meet him at church every Saturday--and I continued to walk to the Lutheran Church every Sunday to meet up with my sister Ruthe.

I observed quickly that Adventists weren't just Bible readers, they were committed Bible students and they also read a lot of religious books with captivating titles like *The Great Controversy*, *Steps to Christ* and *Desire of Ages*. As an avid reader, I enjoyed this new avenue of study. Few of the people that I'd met at the Lutheran church knew anything more than what they'd read in their catechism book. None of them seemed to know scripture. They appeared contented with what the preacher told them from the pulpit week after week. Though I'd attended a lot of churches with friends over the years, none of them were knowledgeable about the Bible. They seemed content without self-searching.

Soon I learned, much to my astonishment, that the change of Sabbath from the seventh-day of the week is easily validated by the observance in 321 A.D. from Saturday to "the venerable day of the Sun" Sunday, by Emperor Constantine on behalf of the Roman Catholic Church, in books at the local library. I didn't need the Bible to prove that change. History records it. Therefore, it isn't an interpretation but a fact. *But why*, I questioned, *didn't all churches, at least the Protestant churches, observe the Sabbath? Why did they worship on a day that history itself shows as obviously giving homage to paganism?* It certainly didn't make sense to me. Some people told me that the commandments were done away with—nailed to the cross. Others said that Christians worship on Sunday because Jesus arose on that day. But nowhere in the Bible does God admonish us to do that. Again, I thought *why would Jesus have admonished us*, in John 14:21, (KJV) "He that hath my commandments, and keepeth them, he it is that loveth me" *if he planned to do away with them--or change the Sabbath day observance?"* And further more I pondered, *who would want the commandments done away with?* It seemed that whomever I talked with agreed that they wouldn't want them done away with either. Only the fourth commandment--the Sabbath--seemed to be a problem with them.

The Bible cleared it for me with Acts 5:29, (KJV) "Then Peter and the other apostles answered and said, 'We ought to obey God rather than men.'" Thus, my choice, I must obey God regardless of my personal, family and social consequences. Little by little I clearly came to comprehend that the Christian life required dedication, not simple acquiescence. My search for God proved to be an experience in tough decisions. Yet I felt a peace I'd never before known in all my life. Joy filled me.

Johnny and I started talking marriage--though it became clear after many discussions that we still held some differing opinions; lifestyle in particular. He said without a doubt that he'd never marry anyone except a Seventh-day Adventist. At this point I figured that regardless if we were to be a couple or not I wanted, indeed, I needed to know more about what and why, the ins and outs of how Seventh-day Adventists believed--and most of all I knew that with all my heart, I wanted to obey God.

Johnny suggested, "The best way for you to really find God is to do some serious Bible study. I know someone who will be glad to give you Bible studies, and to explain to you the points upon which we disagree. Then you'll be able to make an intelligent decision." I said, "Okay, but I want you to go with me to study with my pastor too." He readily agreed.

After attending the Seventh-day Adventist Church for a few weeks, Johnny and I drove to his friend's home for my first in-depth Bible study. Harry and his wife, Ann, set up a projector and screen in their living room to view Bible studies via filmstrips, similar to a movie. Of course we also used our Bibles as we studied. I think I asked a million questions and that first Bible study turned into a midnight oil-session.

That night I learned how to unlock another door--the door of prophecy. This proved to be a whole new, fascinating aspect of religion for me. Daniel 2 captured my attention instantly. I thought, *wait a minute here, I just studied all this in my high school Ancient History classes. Can it be that these kings and kingdoms were prophesied to happen?* As a recent high school graduate and one who especially enjoyed the study of ancient history, King Nebuchadnezzar's dream enthralled me, a dream that distressed him. This dream even stumped his palace wise men. They simply could not interpret what he shared with them. I realized that God's word held much intrigue.

What was the meaning of the magnificent image with a head of gold, chest and arms of silver, belly and thighs of brass, legs of iron, and the feet (ten toes) of iron and clay? God's faithful servant—the Hebrew teenage captive Daniel endowed with the gift of prophecy defined the image for the king as the world kingdoms of Babylon, Grecia, Medo-Persia, Rome, and the 10 nations that would never unite into a major kingdom again until God sets up His kingdom. This dream revealed a view of world powers to rise and fall throughout the course of history: nations yet to come, history yet to be lived. The stone cut out of the mountain that breaks apart the 10 nations obviously represents the Second Coming of Jesus. Amazing facts—all from the Bible!

A clincher text in Daniel 2—at the end of verse 45 read, "The great God has shown the king what will take place in the future. The dream is true and the interpretation is trustworthy." (NIV) Truth and trustworthiness! Confidence in God's word satisfied me.

This introduction to Bible prophecy thrilled my God-seeking heart. It also showed me that there's more to this world than just a human show of nations run by men, that God plans for an indestructible kingdom. By this time, I wanted, I hungered to know more. The pages of the Bible that I'd purchased as an adolescent six years prior got turned a lot. As a result of opening this new door of reading and study my heart filled full with happiness, as I discovered the joy of Jesus, my Lord, throughout Scripture.

The book of Jeremiah pointed out to me that God

planned my life. This revelation infilled me with confidence that God cares for me, as I read in the 29th chapter, verse 11, " I know the plans I have for you, declares the Lord, plans to prosper you and not to harm you, plans to give you hope and a future." (NIV) At that time I didn't know what His plans entailed but I looked forward to His plans because He promised to prosper me with hope and a future free of harm. *What did He have in mind for me?*

Mended Wing

Once
I was as a sparrow with a broken wing
As a voiceless-canary; no voice to sing
Yet God knew my heart-yearning to fly free;
Thus, he set a wind current under me.
I was lifted up to mountain height
Where he showed me His grandeur and might;
And soar I did with song in my breast,
As I flew beyond the eagle's nest.
No limit to the course I'd fly:
His messenger the Dove came by
To show me that my task would be
To praise His name for flying free!

by
betty kossick

Chapter V

"ABBA"

"...he turned the key and unlocked yet another door for me."

The weekly Bible studies drew me like a magnet. During the week, between the appointed studies, I delved into my Bible with gusto. Studying, comparing text with text, and reading with an understanding to consider the context and the setting of a verse proved to be a real eye-opener. I almost forgot about Johnny's agreement to go to my pastor and study with him too. *I'd better get that appointment made, surely my pastor knows how to explain away these discoveries.*

I called to set up an appointment; but my pastor didn't seem his usual friendly self. He firmly said, "No, I won't study with your young man. If he's a Seventh-day Adventist I won't be able to change his mind." My pastor's refusal for at least one meeting confused me. Sorely disappointed, I quit attending the Lutheran Church.

Then, toward the end of summer a surprise drop-in visit from my former pastor found the two of us in deep discussion, "So tell me" he started, "are you still worshipping with the Adventists? I haven't seen you at church services." At that, I opened up like a turned on faucet, sharing all my new Bible discoveries. Innocently, I'd inquire, "Do you know about that?" At every point, he'd answer affirmatively, agreeing with me. He didn't raise his eyebrows or make any attempt to dissuade me. In fact, he seemed intrigued-- and I believe a bit surprised with my new attitude about God and the things of God.

Then I queried, while taking a quick glance at his tobacco-stained fingers, "Do you believe that your body is the temple of the Holy Spirit?"

"Yes, I do," he sheepishly answered while he, too, examined his long, bony fingers.

"Then, why do you smoke? Don't you know that you're killing yourself?"

"You're right, I shouldn't," he agreed. "It's a long-time habit."

"Addiction, you mean?" I insisted.

He nodded affirmatively, glancing away from me.

Then I got a bit bolder, "If you agree with me about what I've been learning, especially about the sanctity of the Sabbath, why don't you teach this to your parishioners?"

He grimaced, but he calmly answered me, "Betty, if I did, they'd all leave the church. It's too hard for most people to change or live such a strict life. You're only an 18-year old girl. I know that you like to dance, you've told me. Adventists frown on dancing, young people won't give up the good times, and older people usually won't either. It will be difficult for you to live the kind of life the Adventists require of their members. I doubt that you can do it--but if you can then you should join with the Adventists."

His words startled me! I replied, "Well, I don't consider that anything I've learned is strict or confining—though at first I thought some things were strange—but why wouldn't I? I'd never known about them! In fact, I feel released. Now, I have honest excuses for not doing some of the social activities and antics that bother me, like the parties. Parties I find lead to foolish behavior. At one such party, I tried drinking beer and smoking. *Nasty stuff!* I want no part of it." Still he provided no valid counsel to convince me to backtrack.

When my pastor left that day, I still considered him a

friend but for sure not my pastor anymore. However, he guided me in a way that I'm sure he didn't intend to. *He turned the key to unlock yet another door for me*--a door of major decision. His agreements, his cautions, and his admonitions convinced me to become a Seventh-day Adventist.

More exciting discoveries awaited me with every turn of the Bible's pages. A text I found in the book of Jeremiah, chapter 29, the 13th verse, warmed my heart. From the time I first read it; I claimed it as a promise from God, "And ye shall seek me, and find me, when ye shall search for me with all your heart." It's the verse I share with other seekers because it is indeed a promise.

Through my studies I learned that I had a Daddy who would never disappoint me, one who desired to be part of my life forever: Abba, my Father, my God. Learning that the word Abba holds the more affectionate meaning of Dad or Daddy, the name Jesus used for God, His Father, provided me with a mother lode of comfort. Now, I really had a Daddy.

The more I learned, in meetings or in my personal Bible study time, the more I wanted to share with others. Soon, Johnny and I started giving Bible studies to others. We finalized our wedding plans. Friends showered us with the usual parties. We also chose to be baptized together to prepare us for our union with Christ and with each other. We chose Christ as the hub of our life.

When we went to the Summit County Court House to obtain our marriage license my mother went with us because I was a month shy of 19, below Ohio's legal age requirement at that time; we needed her signature. At 21, Johnny needed no one to sign for him.

The lady whom we talked to asked me quite bluntly, "Young lady, where is your father? Don't you know that you can't get married without your father's permission and signature?"

Aghast, I told her, "My parents are divorced and he's never supported me. My mother will sign for me."

"If you have a living father, he must sign for you," she insisted firmly.

"No, he won't!" I blurted adamantly, "In fact, if he has to sign, I'll wait until I'm 21 to get married. My mother told me that if he'd help pay for my wedding that he could give me away. I asked him but he told me he couldn't afford it. We're having a simple wedding. If he can't even do that for me, he's not going to sign for me."

At that my mother puffed her cheeks, interrupting, "We'll just see about this! Let's go. We'll talk to Verne T. Bender, the Clerk of Courts."

"It won't do you any good! The law is the law," the woman argued haughtily.

Soon we stood in another office with my mother angrily explaining to Mr. Bender about how the woman refused to prepare a license for us. I shrunk into the circle of Johnny's arm embarrassed about the encounter. Mom told Mr. Bender in a disgusted, testy voice, "We've had a difficult life and her father didn't care enough to ever help." She emphasized to him how she waited for five years to afford a divorce. "During all that time he never helped us in any way," she insisted.

Mr. Bender excused himself and returned with a folder. He smiled at me and inquired, "Would the bride-to-be allow me the privilege of signing for her?" He opened the folder he carried and showed us only one record of a support payment recorded in the eight years since my parent's divorce was finalized. "In my opinion, the man doesn't have any right to sign for you."

Mother looked satisfied, almost smug, as if she'd

won a court case! In a way, she did. Mr. Bender accompanied us back to the woman in the other office. Her furrowed brow revealed her unhappiness with our return. After the completed signing, Mr. Bender obviously wanted to talk with her—alone. Johnny and I-- and Mother--thanked Mr. Bender for his kindness and consideration to me. We left the courthouse, figuring the woman probably got a reprimand.

On April 23, 1950, a year from the day we met, Johnny and I were pronounced man and wife at the First Seventh-day Adventist Church in Akron, Ohio. My brother-in-law "Bud" gave me away instead of my father.

Johnny's home life nearly equaled mine as a child. He came from a home divided both by religion and lifestyle. His father boozed too. His mother, he and his brothers also knew the sorrow of drunkenness. Johnny and I determined that our home wouldn't meet that fate. Though we were probably as poor as the proverbial church mice, we wanted a Christian family—a family with a safe harbor.

Our prayers early on were for children to complete our home. Two years after our marriage, we delighted in our daughter Stephanie's birth. In 1955 our son Kevin's birth added more joy to our home. We dedicated them to the Lord as infants. Johnny's grandmother used the term "golden balls" to describe the joy of children in the home. Our children fit that description.

When our children were very young, I invited my Mom to evangelistic meetings at our church. As she studied, she chose to be baptized. Joining the Seventh-day Adventist Church provided a turn-point with her new faith, providing happier days for the rest of her life.

Johnny's father, who attended a Catholic college preparatory school to study for the priesthood before he met and married Johnny's mother, also became a Seventh-day Adventist. His carousing days ended and his life brightened in his older years.

No matter how tough our financial situation, Johnny and I agreed I'd be a stay-at-home mom while our children were young. I never wanted to be too busy or too tired to be there for their hugs at the end of the school day. So many times as a child I prepared a bologna sandwich for a meal–to eat alone. I don't think that I ever participated in any school function that I didn't possess a heavy heart--unless my mom came. I resolved to be present for my children.

In the early years of our marriage, Johnny worked at a furniture factory. With an inadequate income, Johnny went off to work most days with only pocket change. Regardless, we chose to be faithful with tithe and offerings. We didn't want to rob God. Maybe not our wants but our needs were always met.

From the first week of our marriage we'd kept a budget. The Economics class that I took in high school proved valuable. Quite carefully I distributed each dollar. Many times Johnny worked 16-hour days to keep us going financially but God always provided the opportunity to earn as needed.

Even before I worked outside the home, I found opportunities to earn a few shekels by taking in work at home, like ironing those wrinkles out of other people's clothing. I also put my artistic skills to use and sold designs to the furniture factory where Johnny worked. Of course, we probably shouldn't have married without better employment or savings but we lived like most of our friends did in the 50s. Reared through the Depression, short on finances fit most of us –and we assessed our circumstances as, "Were doing okay."

A couple of years after our marriage the young son of my former Lutheran pastor died. I wrote a letter of sympathy to his parents. I wasn't able to attend the child's funeral but my sister Ruthe did. She told me that the pastor said he'll treasure my letter and he asked her to tell me, "Betty made the right decision." His affirmation meant a lot to me.

As our children grew, I desired to enroll them in church school. But Johnny constantly worried about our finances—and the ensuing tuition. "Impossible," he said. "We can't do it. Public school is good enough." Serious discussions led to unresolved arguments. I despaired for our children. *Will they ever know this privilege*, I pondered. I sought the advice of a Christian counselor about this. He said, "Why are you so concerned? Your children aren't ready to go to school yet. I'm sure it will all work out by then." His counsel proved correct. Johnny eventually agreed and we enrolled our children at the modest school, held in the basement of our church building on West Market Street. Christian education provided a vital part of our lives. Our home, the church, and the church school, became a circle of love, like a big hug for us. Johnny never regretted our decision.

Many Seventh-day Adventists talk about the sacrifice parents make in order to send their kids to denominational schools. For us, we feel that the only real sacrifice is if they do not attend a school where God is the hub. We delighted to see our children learn more than the basic studies. The core of Christian education–God the Father, Jesus the Son, and the Sweet Holy Spirit–meshed in with every subject. Prayer provided as much a part of academics as mathematics for our children.

During these years, we continued to be fully church oriented and Johnny and I enjoyed giving Bible studies to seeking folks. Befriending new believers and inviting friends and strangers home to eat with us on Sabbath, after church service, became an undertaking we enjoyed almost weekly as a family.

When our daughter enrolled at boarding school at Mount Vernon Academy, 80 miles from home, I went to work outside the home for the first time to help pay the school bills. An industrious worker, Stephanie worked hard to help pay the school bills. In order to work, I didn't leave our son Kevin on his own. After school he rode a bus to my workplace and worked at his own job there. Then, when he reached academy age, he also attended Mount Vernon Academy. He, too, worked diligently to keep his tuition paid. I continued at a variety of jobs utilizing my skills with art, organization, and people, including part-time employment as an Ohio Conference Bible worker. But like the good Father He is, Abba groomed me all along to do a special task. Another door waited to be unlocked.

"Commit they way into the Lord; trust also
in Him; and He shall bring it to pass."
Psalm 37: 5 (KJV)

Prayer of Dedication

Father, God, O, make me
as a cathedral for You,
may my heart be as windows
ushering love through
each pane, with dancing colors
of Your kindly peace
so my worship will be
incense to You to increase
my service -- and use my life
and works as pillars;
allow Your beauty within
to glow as lamp stars
to light the house wherein
You dwell that I can be
a refuge of comfort for
those searching for Thee.

Accept my dedication,
O, Lord, I pray

by
betty kossick

*The first
summer
of our
marriage
1950*

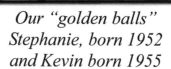

*Our "golden balls"
Stephanie, born 1952
and Kevin born 1955*

Chapter VI

"A WRITER EMERGES"

"For three years I prayed that God would give me something special to do for Him."

All along life's way, God's promises gave me courage in the toughest times--and they affirmed my decision to follow Jesus in the most joyous times. I continued to feel grateful for that pencil given to me years before—the pencil that led me to study God's word.

Over the years, Johnny and I acquired a bountiful friendship garden. Some of the closest in heart are Seventh-day Adventists but a large number are of other denominations as well as non-believers. Sweet are the memories of the good times we've enjoyed with these friends. One of the rewards of these treasured friendships is that the ones formed when our children were at home are also friends of our children. Our children always seemed as happy in their company as were Johnny and I.

Like most families, we experienced our ups and our downs such as testing illnesses, financial straits, and interpersonal family relationships gone awry. At times, both of us felt discouragement. At times, Johnny and I even wondered *is our marriage a mistake?*

Despite our concerns and misgivings, I asked God to give me a special task to do for Him. I didn't specify anything, I just I wanted to be at His disposal. I prayed earnestly toward this end. I desired to be a clean vessel, filled by God.

A few months before my 40th birthday, God set the stage for my special task though I remained totally unaware of His answered prayer for a time. Annually our

Akron church body elected officers to do a variety of duties. These positions, like any volunteer role, are valuable assets to the role of a church and its service both within the church family and in the community. Serving the community always appealed to me. I suppose this occurred as a natural for me because Mom and I received so much help from various community agencies, as I grew up. The "giving back" idea seemed only right.

Since I'd first joined the Adventist church I'd served in various capacities. Though untrained for most of them, a new neophyte role awaited me. The church nominating committee asked me serve as the church Press Secretary; a public relations communicator. My pastor, Marlo Fralick, realized potential in me for that sort of work. He'd observed my social interactions with people in the community, especially as a volunteer for smoking cessation classes that our church conducted in tandem with Dr. John Morley and the City of Akron Health Department. To me, my pastor's confidence seemed ill gotten but he assured me that my abilities fit the task. I surmised, *I was wrong with my early thoughts about Johnny's spiritual convictions, perhaps I'm off base again and my pastor is correct.*

For three years I'd prayed for God to give me something special to do for Him. I'd prayed the supplication of David in Psalm 119:65, 66, (NIV) "Do good to your servant according to your word, O, Lord. Teach me knowledge and good judgment for I believe in your commands." At the same time admonition that I spied on page 65 in the book *Patriarchs and Prophets* also buoyed me for some special service, "The motive that prompts us to work for God should have in it nothing of self-serving. Unselfish devotion and a spirit of sacrifice have always been and always will be the first requisite for acceptable service."

I'd soon realize that God truly answered my prayer to serve Him in a *special* way and that my life course required major new construction. This new task required me to send press releases to area newspapers. How do I do that without training? To add to my dilemma I didn't own a typewriter. A one-finger typist, I typed the hunt-and-peck method. I never studied journalism. Without a notion of what to do, I went to my knees in prayer and asked God to enable me.

The church supplied me with a typewriter, an antiquated Remington; one of those heavy machines with metal rims on the keys that wore the fingers sore with the typing. The church also provided me with an early-style Polaroid camera, typing paper, envelopes and postage stamps. Aside from that, I soloed. But not really, because I'd sorely underestimated the work of the Sweet Holy Spirit. He offered me fine surprises—and profound direction!

To my amazement, everything I submitted to the press came out in print. Our church events filled the religion pages. After a couple of months I responded to an impression to write a letter to Peter Geiger, the religion editor of the *Akron Beacon Journal* to ask him, "Might I be of help to you, is there is any kind of news that you especially want to receive?" The very next day after I mailed the letter he called me. During our conversation he seemed astounded about my role as a novice writer, void of formal training. He commended, "You're doing everything right!" He invited me to come to the newspaper to meet him. I accepted his invitation. I felt compelled to take along the Polaroid camera–and ask him, "May I interview you for a church journal the *Columbia Union Visitor*?" He graciously complied.

Our meeting launched the first of many affirmations that God truly answered my prayer. First, Pete assured me again that I'd been doing everything right. "You're a natural writer, you should be getting paid for your writing," he told me. However, I just accepted his statements as courteous comments, I never expected the special work to grow beyond volunteer status into a profession, as a journalist.

Then he inquired, "How do you share your love for Christ?" I told him of many ways that I shared but recent weeks of distributing pamphlets to homes in our neighborhood especially excited me. Several friends came to our home on Sabbath afternoons to do this. As a result 19 separate homes opened up for Bible studies every Saturday afternoon. Pete's eyes brightened, "Will you write me a story about this and take pictures to submit with the story too?" It seemed to me like an assignment straight from heaven.

Two weeks later the story appeared as a religion page feature. About three months later, "Meeting an Editor" ran in the *Columbia Union Visitor*. Pete assured me, "The interview is your forte."

About this same time, I started writing letters to the editor of *The Signal*, a weekly news journal in the Akron suburb of Canal Fulton where my husband and I lived. I addressed issues that I felt impacted the community. Soon, I received a telephone call from *The Signal's* editor, Allen Etling. He questioned, "Would you consider writing for us as a stringer?"

"What's a stringer?" I asked, revealing my ignorance of journalistic terms. My lack of knowledge with the question didn't deter him, "That's journalism jargon for a freelancer or correspondent writer," he answered.

I explained to him, " I have no journalistic training let alone any degrees." He replied that he'd still like to meet with me, "You've impressed us with your take on various issues. I think you'd work out fine. You know how to write." We set an appointment to meet four days later.

The three nights before the meeting found me sleepless and agonizing, *Dear Lord, what have I done? Am I doing the right thing (even) to consider this meeting? If You don't want me to do this please prevent me from keeping the appointment.* I half-hoped that He'd throw out a roadblock But He didn't. I knew not His pleasant plans for me.

The meeting worked out with thumbs up for both of us. Etling assigned me as a columnist. "But what do I write about?" I queried. "Look out your window and tell us what you observe and what you think about it," he smiled, adding, "I don't think that you'll have any trouble writing a column at all."

That's how I came up with my first column title "The View from Two-Penny Hill" (over the years and in other journals "hill" has been replaced by "haven" according to where we've lived). A sign already hung in front of our home with the name. So it seemed an appropriate column title. I'd designed the sign with my logo as a Christian who writes—the dove of peace, a symbol of communication. My brother-in-law Tom emblazoned the design on heavy wood and Johnny did the finishing. That sign still directs people to our abode, "The Kossick's Two-Penny Haven." And Johnny still refinishes the sign for us when its appearance gets weary.

In addition to column writing, the editor asked to me write feature interviews. My pay: ten cents a column inch. I measured everything published and turned in the tally, then I'd get my pay. Believe me, I worked hard. I didn't even have a car of my own. Because we only owned one car, I worked my hours around Johnny's hours. But I did ask myself, *What business do I have to even consider doing this?* I thought. Yet from the beginning

I loved my work. *Did I have printer's ink in my blood?*

Yet a Bible text in Mark 5:36, (NIV) again gave me confidence, "Be not afraid, only believe." So boldly I told my husband, "I must purchase my own typewriter, I can't use the old church typewriter for my job. I need something dependable." I bought a brand-new electric typewriter. Chagrined, my husband's lack of confidence in my new venture spilled out audaciously, "You'll never earn enough money to pay for that machine." Like me, the discovery of the writer inside me came as a surprise to him—and again, like me he didn't foresee the extent of my journalistic future.

At ten cents a column inch I wrote a lot—but at the end of that first month, I owned the Smith-Corona! Instantly, Johnny became my best fan—and my proofreader. He often chauffeured me to my interview appointments in the evenings after he got home from work. For daytime interviews my friend Marianne, a constant encourager, drove me. She enjoyed the interviews. Several years later I repaid her by teaching writing skills to her when she confessed to me that she'd always hankered to write. Though not professionally employed; now she, too, is a published writer.

My husband and I moved away from the Akron area about 18 months after I started with *The Signal*, when he hired on as an electrician in southern Ohio at Kettering Medical Center. By this time my freelancing branched out to several publications. Soon after our move I joined the *Dayton Daily News*, one of Ohio's largest daily newspapers, as a stringer. I started writing for one zone of the paper's coverage--but within a month the editor said, "We're very pleased with your work, we'd like for you to work all the zones."

Less than four years after we moved to the Dayton

area, we were on the move again: this time with a job transfer for Johnny to California. After 30 years alone Mom remarried but within six years her husband died. A widow, with poor health, she moved in with us and moved west too.

Johnny took over his new duties as the electrical foreman at White Memorial Medical Center, in Los Angeles and I took a job in outpatient billing there. But I quickly found it difficult to write much while working fulltime. The work I did hardly fit into my bag of skills even though I received excellent performance reviews. My heart beat for another task.

By this time I discovered that my capabilities covered many genres of writing. And I'd also learned that versatility in a writer is highly valued by editors. Now I knew I could confidently declare, "I am a writer!" Regardless, of my continued sales and contest winnings, I still felt inadequate because of my lack of formal college training. I passionately enjoyed all my writing opportunities, especially interviewing—especially discovering a person's story. Meeting people, setting up appointments, it all challenged me. I decided to be the best writer possible because I knew God called me to this task.

So, at age 48, I resigned the hospital position and walked through another door, the door of Pasadena City College--where a whole new adventure of creative writing and journalism classes beckoned.

The Writer

Am I writing my own epitaph?
Perhaps – yet
to be known as the writer
then so be it.
The writer of words to bless –
my goal.
Word crafting is a gift
of expression to open.
How dare I not articulate?
Thus, I dip the pen.

by
betty kossick

Chapter VII

"DREAMS DO COME TRUE"

*"My professor looked at me quizzically and inquired,
'Why Haley?'"*

The first two weeks of college classes wore me thin, not because of the studies but because of the flack I got from my classmates. The first day in my Creative Writing class the professor said that she wanted us to read and evaluate the previous year's anthology. She spoke of it in glowing terms, seemingly proud of the job she'd overseen for the college.

Of course, my awareness included the knowledge that the social attitudes in 1980 embraced a let-it-all-hang out perspective. Even so, the anthology sorely offended me throughout. Disappointment engulfed me. What am I into here at this college? . *Where have all the poets gone, I thought? Lord, help me to handle this properly in class,* I prayed.

During our next class session, the professor asked us to give our responses. No one spoke up. She turned to me, the obviously oldest student in the class, and she curtly requested, "Certainly you have an opinion, don't you?"

"Yes, I do, but I don't think you want to hear it," I responded.

"I asked you, I expect an answer," she urged, with an attitude of expectancy.

With every eye on me, though I momentarily flinched at her demand, I started, "I hold to a philosophy about writing, about words, and especially about poetry. I believe that an educated person doesn't need to use gutter words to express oneself. And, as far as poetry goes, my opinion is that low-class verbiage is entirely out of place. As a Christian, I am offended with what I read in the anthology."

With that statement, more than half the class, who were in the 18-20 year-old category, came out of their zonk mode, landing on me with their verbal heels kicking. My fellow students hurled terms such as, "Miss Goody Two Shoes," "Prissy" "Holier than thou," and much worse labels at me. My composure nearly withered. My ears throbbed with my heartbeats. I wanted to flee, to shut their faces and their words away.

The professor seemed a bit smug about the class defending the anthology but she didn't berate me. She did, however, give us an assignment for the next class, making certain that the students knew she considered herself a Bohemian free-spirit. They would not, could not offend her, she asserted. However, the next session provided an opportunity to open a can of pornographic worms. Even she experienced offense after all.

Though I'd prayed before I ever started the classes that I'd somehow be a blessing, my prayers increased with intensity. *Lord, I don't want to make enemies here, but friends.* I made it through the next weeks--and even got good responses to my comparatively Puritan offerings. Then one day after I read my piece "The Little Yellow Rocker" relating my miserable childhood experience, one of the classmates surprised us all by apologizing to me as I finished reading. She came over to me and gave me a compassionate hug.

She confessed that she'd agreed with me the day of the anthology evaluation. Full of shame, she apologized for not defending me. Then another and another admitted the same. This seemed to both shock and please the professor.

I'd previously thought of the professor as my adversary but perhaps not.

When the time came to elect the editorial staff for the new anthology—and the votes were cast-- my name appeared among them! Though surprised, I accepted, with the stipulation that submissions not contain offensive wording. I challenged us to restore worthwhile poetry and prose for our anthology. With their complete agreement, we proceeded.

The finished product received high marks for the college. But the best review came by J.V. Cunningham, professor *emeritus* of Brandeis University. Cunningham, a distinguished literary critic, was selected by PCC as Poet of the Year. His work appeared with ours in the anthology. He wrote, "The whole issue is what one would have no right to expect." Then he mentioned some of the works in particular, and of the poetry he praised mine first. I'm glad I insisted on words of worth for that anthology.

Working on the college newspaper the *PCC Courier* brought back old pleasures to me–getting the story and getting it right. How often I recalled and thought of Aunt Golda's admonition: *the reason we iron is to get the wrinkles out*. More and more I became aware of the importance of self-editing and to appreciate an editor's hard work. Such a lot often fell on me even without the designation. When my classmates found out that I'd already acquired eight years of newspaper writing before I came to PCC, they started coming to me for advice--even with personal problems. Often it opened a door of opportunity to pray with them. As a result, fine friendships ensued.

One day on an assignment to interview PCC's Director of Foreign Students, she asked me to stay by following the interview. Leaning a bit across her massive desk she smiled kindly and said, "I hope you realize that you've left your mark on this college campus." She chuckled and asked, "Do you know that some of the students respectfully call you Professor Kossick?" Another affirmation, another blessing!

Then the day came when Professor Kolts announced that we journalism students needed to decide on the name of the person we plan to interview for our personal class project. It must be someone of note, and include information to prepare three separate articles about that person: a personality profile, an opinion piece, and a breaking news piece. We also needed to suggest a publication to which we'd like to submit our work.

I approached Kolts with my choice. "Alex Haley," I said. " I recently read in *Writer's Digest* that he lives in East Los Angeles. Before I'd moved to the Los Angeles area from Ohio last year, I only dreamed that I'd like to interview him someday but maybe …."

My professor looked at me quizzically and inquired, "Why Haley?"

"Because," I said, " I learned that he was an interviewer long before he delved into his family search and ended up as a Pulitzer Prize winner for 'Roots.' I've read a lot about him but almost everything is like another coverage of his book. I want to take a different route and quiz him on his spiritual roots. His book mentions the church life which influenced him." And, yes, I know the publication I'll send my main story to: *These Times.*

Professor Kolts didn't say, "Go girl." She still looked puzzled. I questioned, "You don't think I can do it do you?"

With a broad smile she replied, "Oh, I have no doubt that you can write the story – but getting the interview, that will be the problem. Don't you realize that with his current popularity he's every journalist's dream? You know, Betty, the Mayor of Pasadena or someone of similar note will do just fine for this project."

"Well, Haley's my dream too--and I'll pray about it. If the Lord wants me to interview him, I'll get an interview." She smiled at me more broadly. *I'm sure she's hoping that I'll snag him! It will be a feather in her cap, too, if I do.* I thought.

Two days later the PCC Courier's editor, Wynona, a young woman of color, came up to me and inquired, "Betty, do you really want to interview Alex Haley?"

"It's my dream," I insisted.

She handed me a folded paper and said, "This will open a door for you." She rushed off. I unfolded it and found a neatly printed address---a post office box number. The instructions noted that I write a brief letter telling Alex Haley why I wanted to interview him and a list of 10 questions to ask him. I'd receive a telephone call if he found interest in my request. I immediately assigned myself my own homework for that night: follow the instructions on the folded paper. I did.

A couple of days later, I'd barely opened the door returning from school when the telephone rang. I answered to a lovely voice, "Hello, Betty Kossick? My name is Jackie Naipo. I'm Alex Haley's Administrative Assistant. Mr. Haley is interested in your request. Would you like to set up an appointment?"

I started thanking God mentally, as I marked my calendar and thanked the cheerful voice of Naipo. Certainly, she delivered great news. She noted, " Mr. Haley is a very busy man and selective about those to whom he grants interviews but he is intrigued with your line of questioning about his spiritual roots. He also expressed a sympathetic bent because you admitted that you're a grandmother, not a starry-eyed teenager."

Then a testing session went into mode for me. Jackie

called several times over the next two months canceling and rescheduling our appointment due to more important engagements. Most of these delays were for high-paying speaking engagements for Haley. These, of course, took precedence for his time.

It became obvious that I'd not be able to complete my project for the class deadline. With summer vacation on tap, *I'll fail the class if I wait for Haley.* My fiftieth birthday approached. I asked the Lord for a birthday present. I also asked my professor for an extension. Granted. By this time Professor Kolts' enthusiasm grew as intense as mine—and my classmates were also anxious for me. This slated Haley interview pumped up the whole class. My classmates cheered me all the way.

On May 25, 1981, one day before my "50" birthday, I sat in Haley's office in East Los Angeles, interviewing him. Before I began quizzing Haley, I told him that mechanical devices make me nervous. I asked him for his patience, as I'd be checking the tape recorder during the interview to be sure it works properly. Haley smiled, patted my hand and said, "Don't worry, you take notes, I'll watch the tape recorder." He did. *What a nice guy!* I mused.

Jackie previously advised me, "The interview is one hour. Another interviewer is scheduled immediately after you." No problem. In that one hour Haley filled my coffer. Only one snag, I'd not be privy to his breaking news. That must go out to the public through other means. But, I thought, *perhaps Professor Kolts will allow me to interview Jackie, she's such an interesting woman. To be the right hand for such an important writer as Haley gives her clout.*

Fortunately, Professor Kolts understood my dilemma and agreed. From the one-hour interview with Haley and a telephone interview with Jackie, I acquired fodder for five stories. The stories were printed in *These Times*, the *Glendale News Press*, (2) and The *Star News* Pasadena (2). Over the years since I've used bits and pieces of Haley's quotes for several articles as well as for this book. Ah! a journalist's mother lode.

Also, I retain a hand-written evaluation of the interview that Haley sent to Professor Kolts, as well as a personal note of appreciation and encouragement that he penned to me. These are treasures of the sweetest kind for this writer.

Another interesting note about the Haley interview: as I went to leave his office, I took notice of a captivating piece of art hanging on the wall, a painting of Haley with his African ancestor Kunte Kinte painted within his heart. A touching piece of artistry--indeed. Haley told me that he received the gift from a Seventh-day Adventist, an artist from Oakwood College. When I said, "Mr. Haley, I'm a Seventh-day Adventist too." His eyes brightened and he squeezed both my hands together tightly, He smiled, "I should have known." He also spoke highly of a young Seventh-day Adventist woman he once employed. Sure enough, the other writer sat waiting, when my time with Haley passed. Yet I'll ever treasure my hour with this gracious man.

Yes, my benefactor classmate's prediction proved right, the folded piece of paper with the P.O. Box number did open a door for me--and a dream came true.

Why pray?

Why do I pray to
a God I can't see?
What does this act
do for Him, for me?

What difference does it make to pray?
to a God so far away?
Ah! that's it to, draw close to Him,
intimate joy, not a whim.
No foolishness making my pleas,
calling, as I'm on my knees.
His answers come in varied ways,
some at once, other times days
or maybe months or even years,
often times with many tears;
but in His time, and in His way
He'll answer me, as I pray.
My heart is softened as I come
with petitions one by one.

Why do I pray to
a God I can't see?
It's a faith thing
between Him and me.

by
betty kossick

Chapter VIII

"OPPORTUNITIES"

"Never be a Jonah, I reasoned."

The same month that I capped my interview with Alex Haley, in May 1981, *Woman's Day* magazine awarded me the Silver Spoon (sterling silver, that is!) Award for a vegetarian menu. *Woman's Day* television channel also featured it. Because of that national coverage, several other news journals interviewed me for stories about me as a vegetarian cook and a free-lance writer. I found out quickly that I'd rather be the one getting the story when it comes to interviews! Regardless, the whole moment of fame route resulted in a fun undertaking.

After Haley, a temporary downer came my way when I realized the need to curtail my college classes. During my 18 months at PCC, I carried a constant A grade, won journalism awards, including first place in news writing judged anonymously by area newspapers editors from such journals as the *Los Angeles Times*, as well as other writing honors; a problem invaded my life. I faced a hard choice.

Mother, who lived with Johnny and me, suffered a stroke. She couldn't seem to regain substantial emotional stability. (We didn't know at the time that she was also developing Parkinson's Disease). All along, she showed her displeasure about me enrolling in college. She fussed when I'd leave home and fussed at me when I returned. She probably still thought I desired champagne taste with beer money but since I was an adult, as well as a grandmother, she no longer said so. I tried to tie her into my work by asking her to proofread my writing. She proofread well--

and I always commended her. Each time she read a manuscript, she waved it at me, pointing out typos with obvious delight. Never once did she compliment my writing. At the same time, her behavior turned more and more erratic and unnerving. As a result this left me dealing with my own emotional weariness.

Only once did Mom seem happy with the interview contacts I made. As I walked in the door, one sunny California afternoon, she oohed, "You got a call today from the actor Robert Young. Here's his telephone number, he wants you to call him." She informed me, quite obviously thrilled, that she'd conversed with the popular movie/ television star, "He sounds very nice, just like he sounds on *Marcus Welby, M.D.*"

Yet for the most part Mom's verbal outbursts and obvious depression intensified. making her more difficult to deal with—and my own emotions frayed. Daily tensions mounted. I didn't realize the extent of it until one day I read an article in *Reader's Digest* titled "Breakdown." The graphic title printed above the article appeared as broken-apart letters. Suddenly, I flinched! I saw myself in that article--and I realized that if I didn't make a change for her sake I might end up in a mental ward. I decided to take what I'd learned during those 18 months at *PCC* and add it to my treasure trove of experiences. Mom needed me more than I needed the classes. I returned to correspondent writing without a degree but certainly with lots of added experience. During my college stint, Professor Kolts proved herself as a real friend--a valued touchstone. When I revealed my decision not to continue with college classes, she understood--and assured me, "Betty, you'll do just fine."

Another factor that made me realize the wisdom of this decision occurred one Sunday morning, when Mom dropped an information bomb on me. I knew very little about my paternal or maternal relatives—and only met a couple of them. So, it shocked me when she told me her mother worked as a correspondent for their hometown newspaper, when my mother and her seven siblings grew up in Pennsylvania. That era didn't produce many female news writers. By this time I'd been a correspondent for more than 10 years, thus; this news astounded me, the news gatherer! I'll admit that I took offense that Mom never told me this before. "Why did you wait 10 years to tell me?" I asked. She just shrugged her shoulders and looked away. Yet I figured it out when she turned back to me and confessed, "I always resented my mother going into her room and shutting the door to do her writing and painting." *And art too?!* I thought. I spent hours with art projects as a child and even into adulthood before I knew a writer dwelt inside of me. Obviously, Mom felt shut out. In fact, she poured out her feelings that she always felt unloved by her mother. I easily surmised: it added up that she probably transferred her long ago feelings of neglect to me as well.

Now, I understood her outward lack of affection to me. In her mind's recall, I represented her mother all over again. I also realized more than ever how much she depended on me emotionally. Obviously, I made the right decision to help Mom but I'll admit I experienced my own feelings of loss.

Though I missed the college classes, my professors and classmates-- and the interesting summer internship I'd served for the public relations department of the college, I didn't miss a stroke with writing. I jumped back into my rowboat.

So I wasn't sailing on an ocean liner but I'd get to the shore. I knew how to use the oars. And this analogy fit me well: Another ever encouraging friend, Louise, shared with me a fascinating observation she made at the Essex Shipbuilding Museum, in Essex, Massachusetts. What she told me, I applied to myself –and I continue to do so. She told me, "Boat building has been a prominent vocation in the Gloucester area for more than 300 years. A boatyard is a part of the museum and this is what happens there: Among the highlights is a room with a 20-foot long steamer box and the frame of a wooden boat. After a thick straight boat plank is steamed, workers wearing thick gloves remove the plank from the steamer, and others start applying clamps at one end. Moving along the plank, at spaced intervals, the clamps fasten the plank to the boat frame; the result is a curved plank that is securely attached."

I related to this plank curving process. I'm being shaped as a writer, to sail through the sea to islands of words: islands of information, of interest, of blessing, of comfort. It's important that I'm pliable. I must bend to the steam and the clamps.

Rejection sometimes comes with writing. I've learned that though I firmly believe God's Sweet Holy Spirit directs me, I remain but a human vessel. God is not telling me directly to write this or that; He only gives me writing opportunities.

Those opportunities often come through people. I feel that God sets people in place for me as buoys of help and encouragement. One of those people, a man named Franklin Hudgins did just that. He edited the *Columbia Union Visitor* when we first met.

Over the years, as I employed my volunteer role, along with my professional work as a writer, preparing press releases for church and school, I always dealt with editors in the mix. Hudgins served as a unique mentor-editor, constantly urging me on as a writer both professionally and as a volunteer. Once I almost gave up--but a call from him came at the right time. From then on, he called me *The Champ*.

While living in southern California I also wrote freelance for the Communication Department of the Southern California SDA Conference. As the Director, Marilyn Thompsen invited me on board. We'd worked together in my capacity as the press secretary of the Temple City Church, so she knew my capabilities. She infused me with even more confidence and remains a friend. At the same time, *Signs of the Times* also contacted me to write a column and features for that publication. I did that until *Signs* merged with *These Times*.

While living in five states I've served as the press secretary in nine of 10 churches—and for most of the associated church schools. I've also been a presenter and teacher for communication workshops in various states. That always excites me because it's another opportunity to help those who are just starting out or to help restart those who allowed their writing oomph to languish.

Early during my development as a writer, I read a quote that I adopted as a personal encouragement, "God gives us opportunities; success depends on the use made of them." *Prophets and Kings*, page 486. Those words told me that I held a responsibility; I'd accepted the role of writer, *Never be a Jonah,* I reasoned. Sometimes I'm still a bit reticent with a new assignment but I accept new writing genres as challenges to be a blessing to me and to others. I must respond to those opportunities as they come for I know that I'll learn and grow from them.

Opportunities still continue daily. Occasionally they unnerve me, just as in the beginning when the request came to write for that weekly newspaper in Ohio. Yet so much joy came and continues to come into my life as a result.

However, if I'd known at the beginning of my career what I'd be expected to do, I fear that I might have reneged at the task. I'd most likely have thought, *It's not possible for me to do it.* Remember, I held no original hankering inside me to write. I simply wanted do something special to honor God. Who expected me to do these things? God did—but in His wisdom He didn't allow me to know until the time he'd chosen. He held a talent in reserve for me because He chose to answer my prayer of service in His timing. Those plans of His included me to be a writer.

About this same time, I selected my personal philosophy wrapped up in one word "Others." As a writer I feel it's important to adhere to a stout philosophy yet with attainable goals. As soon as I meet one goal, I set another. My friends Betty and Bob's son Bob, a psychologist, once said to me, "The way you treat others is the way you treat God." Bob's words always stay with me. In fact, it's this thought that convinced me that my writing is a ministry— to others—for God's glory.

My "Others" philosophy serves as the base for my daily prayer as well, "Lord, bless that stranger I'm about to meet, one who will become my friend. Allow me to be a blessing to someone today." Can you imagine the anticipation I look forward to every day by praying this prayer?

For me it seems that I'm constantly walking through a door of some kind. It might be a small arbor, perhaps a large archway but it's an entrance to something new, another exciting experience. If I don't walk through these doors, I realize that I'll become static.

One of the surprises I've encountered as a writer is that people turn their heads like pivots when they hear the word "writer." Somehow folks seem to think there's a magical aspect to writing. If we're actually brave enough to say, "I am a writer," people expect much of us. An amusing aspect of being a writer is that folks also think writers are rich. Ahem! I know many writers and none of us fit that category.

One of the finest opportunities I've enjoyed as a writer is co-founding *Dayton Christian Scribe (DCS)*, in Dayton, Ohio, along with Lois Pecce. We brainstormed the idea to launch this group after attending a 1978 writers' workshop at Andrews University, in Berrien Springs, Michigan. Launched officially in 1979, DCS celebrates every year since with Christian writers of many faiths, and a roster of as many as 60 members. Some of the writers, like me, remain as correspondent members and over the years some of those correspondents hailed from foreign countries. I enjoyed the honor of being the first president of DCS, then when I returned to Ohio in 1989, I served again in that capacity.

Yet Lois is the cog who keeps the wheels turning for that group because she stayed put--but more because she's faithful. She, like me, wants to build writers for God's purposes. She's a top-notch facilitator. In addition, she's a beautiful friend to all the writers she encounters. The DCS members are a mix from all walks of life. It's thrilling to see them published in an abundance of ways to bless others.

My involvement with these writers instilled in me a courage to teach others what I'd learned as a writer. Andrews University (AU) requested me to teach in summer writers' workshops and give plenary presentations for other writers. Yes, even without any of my own degrees. Interestingly, I've taught writing skills to people with doctoral degrees. Of all the students to whom I've taught freelance writing skills, it was a teenage girl in a class of students whose ages reached into the 70s, during an AU workshop, who rewarded me the most. I always ask my students at the start of a new session of learning, "What did you take way from the last class?" Her answer, "That someday my writing will be a resource for someone else." She caught the vision! She blessed my efforts!

Writers always need encouragement because, as with any career, we don't always stand on the mountaintop. We often must write while traversing the valleys of life. Kermit Netteburg and Bill Garber, both who were faculty members at Andrews University, instilled confidence in many writers, including me. I'll forever appreciate them. Outstanding communicators, more of their kind are needed.

I've enjoyed the good fortune of teaching many students over the years. Dare I call myself a teacher when I don't have the tassels to prove it? Well, all I can say is that when I see one of my student's byline, I know that person sat in my home-based or community-based classes and took away something. Passing the torch along, as I run the race is an immensely rewarding experience. My students bless me immensely—and I always learn from them—each one.

Perhaps I need to correct myself when I say that I've not earned any degrees. All these years I've attended the University of the Holy Spirit. The degree I earned is in Kneeology. One day I look forward to meeting my Master Teacher face-to-face and I can thank Him for answering that long-ago prayer.

As I said before, I'm not a rich writer and I don't ever expect to be--but I am quite wealthy. Sit down with me sometime and I'll tell you all about my friendship garden. Gold and silver grow in it. Unique bejeweled flowers flourish in my garden, like Lois who is a true woman of faith, who holds up my hands long-distance many times with her wise advice and encouragement. My friends are gifts from God to me. Johnny and I even have friends, Lela and Leonard, who are so close in heart that they gave us the key to their home years ago. When we visit with them, it's a little foretaste of heaven for us.

Many of these fine folks evolved as friends because of once being my interviewees. Some of them are friends because they were or are my editors and/or mentors and students. Friendship is a great perk of writing. As I listen, ache, rejoice, and sometimes keep serious secrets with my interviewees and the others--I continue to grow and be a happy woman, full of the joy of Jesus. Today, I'm far removed from the fearful and emotional skirmishes that the bewildered little girl faced in the room with the flowered-wallpaper so long ago.

Seasons of Friendship

Our friendship is like
Whippoorwill song, autumn haze,
Snowstorm hearth glow, spring.

by
betty kossick

Memoirs

Memoirs,
a collection of memories written on paper;
good and bad times captured in words,
thoughts and feelings that only I can express
for they come from my own experience:
the tears and the laughter formed into
sentences for me to reclaim at another time,
when I choose to think on the drama, the trauma,
the sweet joy and the bitter heartache of my life
yet mine is not unique or rare, simply mine alone,
and I find both comfort and remorse as I revisit
memoirs.
For me not to write of life's tender and harsh moments is
to pretend that life is all roses and rainbows
and who in all the world can say that of their life?
Thus, I store my memoirs away in poetic form,
some words that only I will read until my death
though sometimes I am brave enough to write
about events that reveals my very own heartbeats
and those who know me best can hear the timbre,
as they read the words for they are those
who have intertwined their heartbeats with mine:
Memoirs.

by
betty kossick

Chapter IX

"CONSECRATED TO GOD"

"Yes, the hurts of yesterday did come around to work for the good in my life."

Is there a writer anywhere who isn't fascinated with words and their meaning? For me, people's names fit into that category also. With surnames we usually associate a heritage, with given names we sometimes wonder why that one was selected. So when I discovered the meaning of my name Elizabeth, which means "Consecrated to God" it gave added fervor to my desire to bless with my writing. Then, when I add the meaning of my middle name Anna, "He has favored me," it only added to my delight.

As a result of this mindset, I allowed myself to be available for more and more opportunities as they came my way, when Johnny and I moved again for his job transfer to Kansas, then again back to Ohio, then yet again to Cadillac, Michigan. All the while I wrote and wrote and wrote.

A year after we arrived in Cadillac I started writing locally. I wrote for the Chamber of Commerce, also a business magazine in nearby Traverse City, and for a Traverse City television station's magazine. However my main local writing outlet was for the daily newspaper *Cadillac News*. My assignments varied from front-page news to business news. But what connected me to the community in a meaningful way was my weekly feature "Faces in the Crowd," as well as my opinion column.

Though I served as a volunteer for most of my life in one capacity or another since my adolescent years, Cadillac afforded me a larger opportunity to serve others.

However I didn't realize how broadly God allowed my influence for good until I started receiving community awards.

"*Celebrate Women*" is an honor given every year to women in the Cadillac community who are chosen as role models to other women. In 1999, I was one of those selected. The occasion is gratifying since it is used as a fundraiser for *OASIS*, a community service, which provides a safety shelter, for abused women and children. I certainly knew what to speak about for my acceptance. The day my telephone rang with the news that I'd been selected, Romans 8:28 instantly came to my mind, "And we know that all things work together for good …"

The Eagle Award presented by *Listen America* became a treasured trophy too. This came because of my positive writing and community involvement as a role model for youth. And there were other awards, as well such as the *Carroll Award* for Distinguished Service for the community. Why would I desire riches more than such appreciation? *Yes, the hurts of yesterday did come around to work for the good in my life.* The questions I asked as a 12-year old when I turned that pencil round and round so long ago were truly answered.

In addition, I realized that the rest of the verse of Romans 8:28 " to them who are the called according to His purpose" indeed provided a prophecy for me. I knew for a surety that God called me to do something for others, for Him. My writing expanded far beyond words on paper. Now, acutely aware of the influence of my words both written and spoken, as well as my actions as never before; I accepted my writing tasks with even greater appreciation. Daily, my attitude grew more humble and more grateful.

This became obvious, too, in my role as a public speaker with *Toastmaster's International*. When an appeal came to the *Cadillac Toastmaster's* group for speakers to go into the community for the annual *United Way* appeal, I volunteered. My classes in Kneeology continued! I volunteered but what do I say? I knew that I didn't want to parrot the brochures or a canned script. As I pondered, I thought of my mother's story. That's it! From the time she arrived in Akron with her two bundles at the safe haven called Salvation Army, she got by with aid from agencies such as *United Way* for several years. My personal appreciation grew deep roots for *United Way* services, since my mother and I personally received community services help. *Certainly, an appeal from the heart is my key for the task*, I thought. Another door to unlock--to help others.

As I presented the story, the *United Way* Board asked me if I'd agree to do it via video. The next thing I knew I wrote a script, and a *Fox TV* crew converged at my home office for filming. It focused as a news reporter telling of how one woman's struggle and needs were met by *United Way* (which had previous handles like *Community Chest* and *Red Feather Agency* early on). I'd never written or done a televised presentation prior to this--but one take and it worked! The camera crew couldn't believe it. They left beaming. I beamed too. God again blessed.

The seven-minute video caused a stir in town. After being used in-house for businesses, as well as via TV, the response provided a very, very generous financial boost for United Way. Because the community residents, many who were readers of my articles, didn't know about my childhood, it astounded them to learn at the end of Mom's story when I said, "I know this story is true because--I am Elizabeth."

Repeatedly, my community involvement indicated that I was "called" to be a part. Without my early fragmented experiences and subsequent understanding, it's doubtful what I'd offer could be as effective. When I worked as a Bible worker in my earlier adult years this also applied. As I served in that capacity many, but not all, of those I studied with were people from sorrowful home situations. There's something about the old axiom of walking in another's shoes that goes a long way as an effective helper. The pastors, with whom I worked as a Bible worker, appreciated me because I understood some of the needy people in a way they didn't. Not that compassion and care can't be well provided by those who haven't experienced the sordid side of life—but obviously my experience served as an asset to help others.

Remember when I first stood on that box as a five-year old and learned to iron clothes? Through all the years afterwards I realize that I applied those ironing skills to everything I did. I determined to iron out the wrinkles. It paid off. Aunt Golda was no witch. A better name: earth angel. At least, she earned that designation from me.

Another aspect of ironing that helped me; when I struggled with problems, I ironed! If something upset me, I'd take out my frustration on the ironing board. The ironing board, the items to be ironed, the iron and I often spent enough time together to resolve any conflicts I faced. Smile! It really worked.

Johnny and I thought that when we moved to Cadillac, we'd always stay there. However, another move waited in store for us to go to Battle Creek, Michigan. Our son took the position as principal of Battle Creek Academy and the family asked us to move on with them. We faced medical problems at the time and it seemed best. Yet part of my heart remained in Cadillac and the following example is one of the reasons.

At *Cadillac News*, Mark Lagerway, the first editor

I worked with there, was a joy to work with. When he decided to leave the news-making realm and return to teaching, he called me into his office. He surprised me when he apologized for waiting for a year to take me on to the newspaper. Then he really surprised me by saying this, "The best thing I've done for this newspaper and the community is have you as a part of *Cadillac News*." Another proof for me that God answered my long-ago prayer. The editor who followed Mark, Matt Seward, also became an encouraging friend as did as the owner of *Cadillac News*, Tom Huckle.

In Battle Creek I didn't work for the local press, instead I returned to my original area of public relations, writing both as a volunteer for *Battle Creek Academy*, and later hired on as the director for public relations for *Battle Creek Lifestyle Heath Center*. However, my writing skills were on tap daily to perform my tasks. Though growing older, there seemed no retiring from the task for writing. I even searched the scriptures and did not find a biblical reason to retire.

Unexpectedly, another opportunity came for Johnny and me. Neither of us are winter advocates, so we moved on to the hamlet of Zephyrhills, Florida. Within two months I applied as a stringer with the *Zephyrhills News* and they took me on a month later. Then the editor asked me to write for its sister newspaper *East Pasco News*, as well. Shortly afterwards the two papers merged as one. I'm slated as a feature writer, including my weekly "Faces Around Town" and "Faces Around East Pasco" and a weekly commentary "The View from Two-Penny Haven." Sounds familiar? It harks back to my very beginning in newspaper writing, doesn't it? I find every day rewarding. None of this is anything unusual except that as I write this I'm 75 years old--and some people think it odd that I don't want to retire--and at the same time they beg me not to. Yes, I do have fans but whether they know it or not they're really fans of the Lord.

My editor, Gary Hatrick, a fellow Christian knows that I believe I can only do what I do through God's direction and mercy. He gave me a gift, a rock (of course to represent Jesus the Rock of Ages) designed with grapes and vines with the text from John 15:1, "I am the vine, you are the branches. He who abides in me, and I in Him, bear much fruit, for without me, you can do nothing." I'm extra blessed to work for him. He understands where my help comes from. The last seven words of the text tell it all.

In addition, I also freelance for a variety of publications by submission and assignment—as I get the time. And by request of another encourager, Martin Butler, the associate director for the communication department, I write a column, for the Florida Conference of Seventh-day Adventists communicator's newsletter, "A More Excellent Way." He and his team of Lee Bennett and Gladys Neigel's expectations of me never allow me to think old. Helping other communicators, providing an impetus for them, gives me true joy.

The extra special interviews continue. An interview with Retired General H. Norman Schwarzkopf, the beloved military leader, who led America through to victory in the famed Gulf War, allowed me the privilege of praying with him in August 2006, following an interview with him.

About six months before interviewing The General, I enjoyed the privilege of flying 5,000 feet in the air in a sailplane with a quadriplegic pilot, to get a story about "Freedoms Wings.'" And just prior to that assignment I did something as part of writing an article that I never expected to do this side of heaven: I petted a baby lion, named Mufasa. In fact, I adopted him. He's as handsome as a male lion gets. I really never know what a day will bring with my writing. I've found that age is no barrier to getting the story.

I plan to continue on as a writer. I'd like to celebrate in 2031 as a working journalist at age 100. But since I'm a believer in the Second Coming of Jesus, I'd rather see that glorious event happen—soon--and work as a heavenly scribe instead--if that's what He's planned for me.

Though my parents didn't know my name's spiritual meaning as "consecrated to God, " or "favored of God," I'm glad that my paternal grandmother and her sister were named those names, so that they became my inheritance. I never knew my grandmother, nor any of my grandparents except my mom's father (and I only saw him twice). Yet I'm sure that Abba designed me to possess a name with fine meaning, so that I'd live up to it, a spiritual goal for myself. I am a writer, I am a miracle--and I am blessed!

Petition

Words on swift wind-wings
Heard by God's listening ear:
Eager, ardent praise

by
betty kossick

My husband Johnny photographed me and
General Norman H. Schwarzkopf (Retired),
following an interview, August 13, 2006

Chapter X

"WHAT OF THE PENCIL?"

"One situation could have left my life in tatters, the other led me on to my joy in Jesus."

As I write, my week is filled full. Filled with what? Writing, of course. Each time I receive a writing assignment or I get an idea to write and submit to some journal I'm again in awe of what my Lord gave me to do. In excess of 35 years (as of 2006), I've been writing press releases, some thousands by now in a volunteer capacity for church, school or community service organizations, and as an employed journalist. I've written articles, short stories, newspaper and magazine columns, poetry (more than 500 poems), scripts, devotionals, newsletters, et cetera. During this time I've gone through the end years of rearing teenagers, grandmotherhood (those wonderful, wonderful grandkids), and now I'm a great-grandmother. My active life continues to give me fodder for my writing.

I've experienced the good fortune to win writing awards and contests. People of international fame shared their time with me. I've lived a bit vicariously by enjoying the privilege of interviewing people who sat in the company of kings and world rulers. They allowed me the unique experience of listening to their stories. Best of all they trusted me to tell their stories honestly. They gave me something of themselves. Some even gave me--and some still do-- a portion of their hearts. I dearly value their notes of appreciation as well.

One interviewee in particular, astronaut Colonel Jim Irwin, a fellow Christian, signed a hand-printed letter to me written on a flight to England this way, "Your grateful brother from the Moon,' Jim Irwin, Apollo 15. Irwin died suddenly four months later. I felt I'd lost a lifelong friend. His letter will ever remain one of my treasures.

Would I have met these internationally known people in any other capacity? Not likely. I remember when a professional friend of mine told me that he saw Alex Haley at a book signing. He felt shy to approach him, and wanted to say more than just, "Please sign my book." So he used my name as an opening wedge. Haley smiled and said, "Yes, I remember Betty well. She interviewed me." Haley didn't forget me, though a few years passed since the interview. It's nice to be remembered, isn't it?

One thing that I want to make clear after all is said about meeting and interviewing the "greats" is this, however interesting their stories, none are any more meaningful to me, as the writer, than the next-door neighbor stories I've gotten.

Daily, I think about that pencil given to me by my teacher back at Lincoln School, in Akron, Ohio. And I thank God. Without a doubt, the best tool to get my attention, to prick my mind with Romans 8:28 needed to be a writing tool. It seems Providential, doesn't it? I've often referred to it as the "powerful persuasive pencil." Yet another teacher also enlarges my story. This book is not complete without mention of her influence.

Miss Mary Riblet took me under her wing the first day I entered her classroom at Akron's South High School. At least she made me feel special from the start. I vocalized about my plans to study commercial art. At the time, a career as a commercial artist or fashion designer seemed perfect goals for me. Thus, she probably thought *Ah! Ha! Here's a 'live' one I can groom.* She did.

Her requests came often, "I'd like for you to enter

another contest." Contest entering took more time than regular class time. It demanded added discipline to the undertaking. Miss Riblet knew the rewards carried more than first-place ribbons. The expanded effort adds resiliency to one's character. I'm sure that the discipline helped develop my stick-to-it-iveness as a freelance writer, even life in general.

I usually won in some capacity: feathers for my cap, her cap: and for the school's cap. But sometimes a contest required expenses that I couldn't afford. Miss Riblet paid the cost for me. She wanted me to win. Yet my college dreams fizzled due to no home encouragement. Mom just stayed stuck in the champagne taste/beer money mode. I obviously didn't have enough confidence back then that I might do it without her consent yet I really did want a family of my own. I needed a real belonging.

When I told Miss Riblet that I planned to marry instead of going to college, she gave me this advice," I wanted to see you succeed as an artist. you have the talent. But I know your yearning and need to have a family life. Make marriage your career. Don't try to do it all."

I kept in touch with Miss Riblet at least at Christmas time each year. I told her about my hopes and dreams as a wife and homemaker, and as a mother. She rejoiced for me, always encouraging.

As I learned to appreciate Bible study more and more, by now teaching my own children, I came across a text that made me think of Miss Riblet. It's another Romans gem, in chapter 12: 7, 8. "...if it is teaching, let him (her) teach; if it is encouraging, let him (her) encourage, if it is contributing to the needs of others, let him (her) give generously..." NIV.

With the erection of a new South High School, she asked me to come to see her new classsroom. As I walked into the room she introduced me to her present students with obvious pride. Then, she went to a cupboard to retrieve a heavy stack of artwork. She spread it out and asked the students to examine it.

I stood astounded! She'd kept all my award-winning artwork. The students oohed and aahed! She beamed and said, "Mrs. Kossick was one of my very best students."

With a tight throat, I felt sick at heart. I felt that I'd let her down. One of her best and I didn't follow through. I couldn't stifle the tears. As if she read my mind, she noted, "You didn't disappoint me because you've made yourself a fine Christian family."

I continued to keep in touch with Miss Riblet. As our family grew, we sent out annual holiday letters. She always wrote back with her beautiful penmanship and said how much she enjoyed every letter of mine. She's actually detailed parts of them.

"Your letters are so different, like a story. I always thought you should be an artist, but perhaps after the children are grown, you should be a writer."

A writer did emerge. Thus, she read some of my early work before she took residence in a nursing home. We continued to correspond and I'd occasionally send her some published items. When her letters stopped, I wrote to the nursing home director to inquire about her. His reply told of her death. He added, "She always spoke about her students. She'd never married. You and all her students were her life." She really fit that Bible text didn't she? She did the Lord's bidding by encouraging, teaching, and giving generously.

Without a doubt Miss Aslan and Miss Riblet greatly influenced my life. The lot of encouragement fell to them. They helped to pick up the pieces of my humpty-dumptyness. But the Master Teacher patiently waited to give me a task to do to glorify His name. I believe he reserved my writing career for the time in my life when I could best serve Him, a time in my life when I needed a balm for a personal heartache. Is there any more wonderful physician for any kind of pain than God?

I'm a great distance from that flowered-wallpaper room where trauma once reigned in my life. I'm a long way from the day I received the pencil too. *One situation might have left my life in tatters; the other led me on to my joy in Jesus!*

So was the Bible text true for me? "And we know that all things work together for the good to them that love God, to them who are the called according to His purpose." My answer is a resounding, "Yes."

Many times during these years, I've heard other people say that Romans 8:28 is their favorite Bible text and I always wonder about their stories. Do they have a story like mine? I know that I'm not alone. My story might seem paled compared to others. But whatever their stories, or maybe it's your story, I'm sure that it's something of interest. Indeed we're a bevy, those who discovered that the Word gave us hope to see us through a dark valley, perhaps many dark valleys. It's doubtful that anyone chose this verse for any small reason. The verse declares too much.

So why not examine that text together from the King James Version? "And we know that all things…" That's profound. All means that everything is included doesn't it?

"Work together for good…." Remember how I couldn't believe anything good could come from my life? What do you think? The word "good" comes from the root word for God. I do believe God reigns in my life.

Lets' say it this way "work together for God."

Aha! It gives me happy goosebumples to think I can work for God. I'm His servant.

"To them that love God..." I didn't know about loving God when I first read the beginning of this text. However, my curiosity about God drew me. Now I know what loving God means and that's what gives me my joy in His Son, my joy in Jesus!

"To them who are the called…" As a 12 year-old I didn't comprehend the idea of what being 'called' meant. Yet my search taught me. That pencil became a tool to woo me unto Him.

"According to His purpose." I am a part of God's purpose; otherwise, He wouldn't have called me. I can't think of anything more wonderful, more exciting, more delightful than being called according to His purpose. Can you?

Another Bible text that I often offer as a prayer of thanksgiving to my Jesus is one that was written by the Apostle Paul, "I thank Jesus Christ our Lord, who has given me strength that He considers me faithful appointing me to His service," I Timothy 1:12, NIV.

When one writes about one's own life, it is very easy to color the picture. Recall isn't always perfect. Yet some scenes are unforgettable, even to the smallest detail, while others are like vapors. With a difficult story, it's tempting to gloss over the truth. It's hard to go naked before the reader.

However Jesus wrapped me in a warm robe many years ago. The Giver of that robe makes it possible that I can share with you, how a little girl, who was born into an emotionally scarred family, found a mighty Guide. He infused my thoughts as I grew into womanhood with a large philosophy of just one word "Others." Through the gift of writing, that philosophy enlarged to be a blessing to me—and I've been assured for the others as well. Though my life began in an aura of darkness, it is by His mercy that I now walk in Light.

To borrow from another writer/editor, Stephen Chavez, who comments this way about stories from real life, …"don't be bashful, tell others your stories, because they're not only your stories; they're His stories also." So, I simply share this story to reveal the joy of Jesus and to tell the world that I'm a daughter of Abba, my Daddy.

I plan one day, when this world is past, to meet the heavenly Trio; to thank my Abba, to thank my Savior Jesus, to thank the Sweet Holy Spirit who gave me guidance-- and I hope also to thank my teacher for the pencil. Won't she be surprised? Yet perhaps not; I rather think that the day she gave her students those pencils, she prayed for someone to discover God.

Glory Task

When Jesus comes
and we're caught up
to meet Him
in the air –
Then on through galaxies
and face to face
with our Father.
Do you wonder
what your task will be
to serve His kingdom?
I hope a quill
is my tool,
a pen
to glorify Him.

by
betty kossick

Epilogue

Confession time. I didn't want to write this book. Oh, I don't mind writing snippets of the life as I experienced it. After all, for years I've written commentaries for newspapers and magazines. That makes a writer extremely vulnerable. I remember when I wrote my first column, a reader said, it amazed her that I shared my family's doings, as well as my feelings with my readers. Yet, for the most part, such writing is more of light-hearted incidents. Sharing so much, as a book requires, especially one that starts out with the issue of domestic violence presented me with a major decision. To delve deep and share more, perhaps might be more than I felt comfortable doing. Yet I did.

Of course, there are parts of my life that aren't written here, I didn't want to be maudlin with the overwriting of pain. However, for the large part I took snapshots of a little girl's life which seemed destined to trail through a dark valley, seemingly far from heaven's portals--and I've shown her as a grown woman whose destiny is heaven bound: my life, my destiny.

Before I bid you adieu, I want to tell you that the day my mother died, my father called me to convey his sympathy. Though he didn't say so, he sounded grief-stricken.

His voice stayed in my mind, so I called him back the next day. I told him that I'd forgiven him when I found Abba. He said, "I'm glad to know." He no longer depended on the bottle but he'd paid a high price for the years that he did. He lost a family, as well as the leg that smashed the little yellow rocker. Amputation was necessary, due to poor circulation; the cost of drinking and smoking for so many years.

At his funeral, four months later, his pastor said, "Jake's biggest regret was that he wasn't the father he should have been to his daughter Betty Ann." Such wasted years for us.

I ventured into this undertaking because others urged me to do so. I put it off until Dr. Darryl Opicka and his wife Annajean insisted that I must. Then, as I wrote, it became urgent for me to share how locked doors don't have to hold us in, we can be free of the snares in our life—to go on and know a life of freedom, freedom acquired by learning such Bible texts as the 25th Psalm, verse 15, (NIV) "My eyes are ever on the Lord for only He can release my feet from the snare."

My freedom is in Jesus Christ. My joy is in Jesus! I found it when I discovered that Romans 8:28 was a promise to me, "And we know that all things work together for good, to them that love God, to them who are the called according to His purpose."

The unlocked doors gave me life abundantly! I pray that what you've read in this book encourages your own walk with God, that you, too, know His joy abundantly. Thus, my signature message is Joy in Jesus!

Final Word

As this book ends, I must add a special "thank you." *Beyond the Locked Door* came about as a result of someone discerning potential in me as a writer—and encouraging me to pursue that avenue. That person is Marlo Fralick, a former pastor of mine--and a friend indeed. His early encouragement led me to where I am today. And much thanks goes to the nominating committee of the Seventh-day Adventist Church in Akron, Ohio who voted me into the position as Press Secretary 35 years ago. That election sent me on my way to become a journalist. God allowed Marlo Fralick and those who served on that committee to be a part in answering my prayer of service.

Recently a writing student of mine, who is a new a sister-in-Christ, Margaret Duran, introduced me to Cynthia Holden who did the layout work for me for the publisher. I'm beholden to Cynthia for her excellent work. She and I enjoyed designing the book cover. The skeleton key in the lock is a digital photo I took of the original skeleton key that I found in my mother's belongings after her death. Cynthia skillfully inserted it into the lock.

In this era of technology it amazes me that as I write in Florida, Cynthia laid out the book in Virginia for the publisher in South Carolina. Isn't God amazing?

At every turn of writing this little book, I discerned God's guidance. It is my prayer that others who were on the dark side of the locked door, will, like me, experience the light that shines through the unlocked door and guides into a life of joy and service. For others who are fortunate enough not to hold such somber memories, I pray that the book inspirits you in other ways. We are all a part of God's fabric to help and encourage one another.

"I thank Christ Jesus our Lord, who has given me strength, that He considered me faithful, appointing me to His service."
1 Timothy 1:12 (NIV)

Made in the USA